DATE DUE

THE ONE TRUE
PLATONIC HEAVEN

ALSO BY JOHN L. CASTI

Gödel: A Life of Logic, the Mind, and Mathematics (with Werner De Pauli)

Paradigms Regained: A Further Exploration of the Mysteries of Modern Science

Five More Golden Rules: Knots, Codes, Chaos, and Other Great Theories of 20th-Century Mathematics

The Cambridge Quintet: A Work of Scientific Speculation

Would-Be Worlds: How Simulation Is Changing the Frontiers of Science

Five Golden Rules: Great Theories of 20th-Century Mathematics—and Why They Matter

Complexification: Explaining a Paradoxical World Through the Science of Surprise

Searching for Certainty: What Scientists Can Know About the Future

Paradigms Lost: Tackling the Unanswered Mysteries of Modern Science

THE ONE TRUE
PLATONIC HEAVEN

ALSO BY JOHN L. CASTI

THE ONE TRUE
PLATONIC HEAVEN

A SCIENTIFIC FICTION ON
THE LIMITS OF KNOWLEDGE

JOHN L. CASTI

Joseph Henry Press
Washington, D.C.

Joseph Henry Press • 500 Fifth Street, N.W. • Washington, D.C. 20001

The Joseph Henry Press, an imprint of the National Academies Press, was created with the goal of making books on science, technology, and health more widely available to professionals and the public. Joseph Henry was one of the early founders of the National Academy of Sciences and a leader in American science.

Any opinions, findings, conclusions, or recommendations expressed in this volume are those of the author and do not necessarily reflect the views of the National Academy of Sciences or its affiliated institutions.

Library of Congress Cataloging-in-Publication Data

Casti, J. L.
  The one true platonic heaven : a scientific fiction on the limits of knowledge / John L. Casti.
    p. cm.
  ISBN 0-309-08547-0
  1. Science—Philosophy. 2. Knowledge, Theory of. I. Title.
  Q175.C4339 2003
  501—dc21

                                2003002279

Drawings by Tony Cavazos and Van Nguyen

CONTENTS

PREFACE

Like my earlier work *The Cambridge Quintet,* this book is not a novel; but it is a work of fiction, what I like to call "scientific fiction." The Japanese term for this kind of work is a *shōsetsu.* Such a work, while containing elements of fiction, is more like a chronicle than a typical novel. In this case, it is an attempt to convey, partly in fiction, partly in fact, some of the intellectual issues associated with the dawning of the computer era.

The principal conflict explored here is the problem of the limits to scientific knowledge. Are there questions about the world around us that are *logically* beyond the power of the scientific method to satisfactorily resolve? Here I emphasize logical barriers, since it is manifestly evident that there are many practical, political, moral, and other reasons why we cannot know as much as we'd like about the scheme of real-world things. For instance, we will very likely never know of the existence or nonexistence of a band of angelic swans inhabiting a planet circling the star 61 Cygni. But that is a practical, not logical, limit to what we can know—it's very time consuming and expensive to travel to and explore that planet, if it even exists. This volume explores the degree to which such a limit to the power of science, if it exists at all, is bound up with our ability to carry out computations.

This issue is explored here within the framework of the computer project promoted by John von Neumann at the Institute for Advanced Study in Princeton, New Jersey, shortly after the Second World War. As this story unfolds, a number of great thinkers from that period—Albert Einstein, J. Robert Oppenheimer, Wolfgang Pauli, Hermann Weyl, and others—weigh in with their views. Not the least of these towering intellects was the mathematician, Kurt Gödel, whose work on the logical limits to mathematics, not to science, forms the backcloth to much of the drama presented here. Interestingly, Gödel's own strange positioning within the intellectual and administrative hierarchy at the Institute presents a second type of conflict: the conflict between human personalities and intellectual accomplishments. That story too unfolds in these pages.

A very important caveat: For the sake of exposition, I have exercised considerable literary license in moving people and events in this story from their actual time and occurrence to a different time or place. The story presented here nominally takes place around spring of 1946. However, J. Robert Oppenheimer did not become Director of the Institute until 1947, Kurt Gödel was not promoted to Professor in the School of Mathematics until 1953, but I've moved both events back in time for the sake of the story. And so it goes. Thus, while I have tried to maintain as much accuracy as possible in accounting for scientific and philosophical ideas in the air at that period, the reader should not take this volume as a work of historical scholarship. I reemphasize that it is a work of fiction. And in works of fiction real-world events and times are often stretched for the sake of the story. Those knowledgeable about happenings in Princeton at the time of this book will see that that is the case here; others won't care. And, to the best of my knowledge, none of these temporal "migrations" harms the real content of the discussions the participants have in these pages. In any event, the book's Epilogue corrects these achronologies and gives pointers to further reading on these and other matters discussed in the body of this narrative.

In this latter connection, I want to draw the reader's attention to the wonderfully readable book, *Who Got Einstein's Office* by Ed Regis (Addison-Wesley, Reading, MA, 1987). Not only does Regis get the chronologies right, he gives a stirring nonfictional account of many of the events and personalities treated here in fictional form. Moreover, I have taken the liberty of borrowing one of the chapter titles from Regis's volume to use as the title of this book.

A word of thanks to three people without whose untiring efforts this book would still be in my computer. The first is Gregory Benford, who served as my advisor and general scourge on matters of both literary style and scientific content. Those familiar with both his award-winning science fiction novels and his pioneering work on space science will realize that I am a very poor pupil. But he tried. And I learned a lot, even if it doesn't always show. Many thanks, Greg.

Next is Jack Copeland, a philosopher of minds and machines, whose eagle eye and vast knowledge of mathematical logic and the theory of computation, as well as its history, saved me from a number of embarrassing, misleading—and in some cases, just plain wrong—statements.

Finally, a deep bow and tip of my hat to the book's editor, Jeff Robbins, who always helped and never hindered. His constructive criticism and insistence on getting it right, coupled with the kind of encouragement that every author needs when it really counts, turned a long project into a short book, but one that can be seen as a coherent *book* and not a rambling collection of remarks. As Gertrude Stein once said, "Remarks are not literature." Neither is this book. But it's a far better story than it had any right to be as a result of Jeff's unstinting efforts.

JLC
Santa Fe, NM
December 2002

DRAMATIS PERSONÆ

John von Neumann (1903–1957): Hungarian-American mathematician who made important contributions to the foundations of mathematics, logic, quantum theory, meteorology, science, computers, and game theory. He was noted for a phenomenal memory and the speed with which he absorbed ideas and solved problems. In 1925 he received a B.S. diploma in chemical engineering from the Eidgenössische Technische Hochschule in Zurich and in 1926 a Ph.D. in mathematics from the University of Budapest. His Ph.D. dissertation on set theory was an important contribution to the subject. At the age of 20, von Neumann proposed a new definition of ordinal numbers that was universally adopted. While still in his twenties he made many contributions to both pure and applied mathematics that established him as a mathematician of unusual depth. His *Mathematical Foundations of Quantum Mechanics* (1932) built a solid framework for the new scientific discipline. During this time he also proved the minimax theorem of game theory. He gradually expanded his work in game theory, and with coauthor Oskar Morgenstern he wrote *Theory of Games and Economic Behavior* (1944).

In 1930, von Neumann journeyed to the United States, becoming a visiting lecturer at Princeton University; he was appointed professor there in 1931. In 1933 he became one of the original six mathematics professors at the newly founded Institute for Advanced Study (IAS) in Princeton, New Jersey, a position he kept for the remainder of his life. He became a U.S. citizen in 1937. During the 1940s and 1950s, von Neumann was one of the pioneers of computer science. He made significant contributions to the development of logical design, advanced the theory of cellular automata, advocated the adoption of the "bit" as a measurement of computer memory, and solved problems in obtaining reliable information from unreliable computer components. Moreover, his involvement attracted the interest of fellow mathematicians and sped the development of computer science.

During and after World War II, von Neumann served as a consultant to the armed forces, where his valuable contributions included a proposal of the implosion method for making a nuclear explosion and his espousal of the development of the hydrogen bomb. In 1955 he was appointed to the Atomic Energy Commission and in 1956 he received its Enrico Fermi Award. His many and varied scientific contributions made him one of the last generalists among contemporary scientists.

Albert Einstein (1879–1955): German-American physicist who contributed more than any other scientist to the twentieth-century vision of physical reality. In the wake of World War I, Einstein's theories–especially his theory of relativity– seemed to many people to point to a pure quality of human thought, one far removed from the war and its aftermath. Seldom has a scientist received such public attention for having cultivated the fruit of pure learning.

By 1909, Einstein was already recognized throughout German-speaking Europe as a leading scientific thinker. In quick succession he held professorships at the German University of Prague and at Zurich Polytechnic. In 1914 he advanced to the most prestigious and highest-paying post that a theoretical physicist could hold in central Europe: professor at the Kaiser-Wilhelm Institute in Berlin. Although Einstein held a cross-appointment at the University of Berlin, from this time on he never again taught regular university courses. He remained on the staff at Berlin until 1933, from which time until his death (1955) he held an analogous research position at the IAS.

Until the end of his life Einstein sought a unified field theory whereby the phenomena of gravitation and electromagnetism could be derived from one set of equations. Few physicists followed Einstein's path in the years after 1920. Quantum mechanics, instead of general relativity, drew their attention. For his part, Einstein could never accept the new quantum mechanics with its principle of indeterminacy, as formulated by Werner Heisenberg and elaborated into a new epistemology by Niels Bohr. Although Einstein's later thoughts were neglected for decades, physicists today refer seriously to Einstein's dream—a grand unification of physical theory.

Kurt Gödel (1906–1978): Austrian-born, American mathematician and logician. He is best known for his undecidability theorems, which state that any rigidly logical mathematical system contains questions that cannot be proved or disproved on the basis of the axioms within the system. These results were an epochal landmark in twentieth-century mathematics, indicating that mathematics is not a finished object, as had been believed. His proof first appeared in a German mathematical journal in 1931. This paper ended nearly a century of attempts to establish axioms that would provide a rigorous basis for all of mathematics. Gödel became a member of the faculty of the University of Vienna in 1930, where he belonged to the school of logical positivism. In 1940 he emigrated to the United States; he was a professor at the IAS from 1953 to his death.

In addition to his work in logic, Gödel had a strong interest in physics and found a solution to Einstein's field equations that implied a universe in which time travel was possible. He spent the last two decades of his professional life in concentrated study of the philosophy of Leibniz and was deeply concerned with metaphysical and theological questions regarding the existence and nature of God.

As a result of a childhood bout with rheumatic fever, Gödel was always preoccupied with his health; he spent the final years of his life in what some believed to be a paranoiac obsession over it, even wearing heavy sweaters and an overcoat on the hottest summer days. Fearful of being poisoned by gases from his refrigerator, Gödel eventually refused to eat and died from self-starvation in Princeton in 1978.

J. Robert Oppenheimer (1904–1967): One of the most influential American scientists of his day. He is renowned for his leadership in developing a strong tradition of theoretical physics in the United States, his direction of the laboratory that fashioned the atomic bombs used in World War II, and his prominent role as a government advisor on military weapons and policy in the postwar period.

After graduating from Harvard University in 1925, Oppenheimer toured European laboratories and institutions for four years just as the theory of quantum mechanics emerged. At Cambridge University he quickly grasped the value of the various mathematical techniques developed to explore this new approach and showed how certain atomic and molecular characteristics could be derived. At the invitation of Max Born, Oppenheimer went to Göttingen in 1926, where he received his doctorate the following year.

World War II turned Oppenheimer's energies to a new line of research. He and others recognized that an explosive chain reaction could be sustained in nearly pure fissionable material (uranium-235 or plutonium) with fast neutrons. In 1942 he was asked to coordinate an investigation into this reaction. As part of the Manhattan Project, research and development work on the atomic bomb was centralized at a remote laboratory in Los Alamos, New Mexico. Even his critics concede that Oppenheimer, as director of the laboratory, performed brilliantly in developing the atomic bomb.

In 1947 Oppenheimer moved to Princeton as director of the IAS. Until 1952 he served as chairman of the board of scientific advisors of the U.S. Atomic Energy Commission (AEC); in 1949 the board rejected a proposal to initiate a program to manufacture hydrogen bombs. Because of his influence on the AEC, his sharp tongue, his sometimes controversial views on military strategy, and his belief in arms control, Oppenheimer incurred the enmity of various members of the military, politicians, and scientists who advocated fusion bombs and a larger strategic arsenal.

Lewis L. Strauss (1896–1974): In the first dozen years of the atomic age, few men played a more pivotal role in shaping American nuclear policy than the former banker Lewis Strauss. An ardent champion of the hydrogen bomb, he was also a strong believer in the importance of maintaining a large nuclear stockpile. His appointment to the United States Atomic Energy Commission (AEC) in 1946 (an agency he chaired from 1953 to 1958) meant he was well placed to influence both President Truman's and President Eisenhower's decisions on nuclear issues and to oversee the atomic-related activities of all federal agencies.

The thorny, owlish-looking Lewis Strauss started out life as a traveling shoe salesman working for his father. He later became an incredibly successful investment banker. By the time he left Wall Street to join the AEC, he was earning a million dollars a year. His new government appointment required him to give up all his business interests, which he told an interviewer, made him feel "like a man who is amputating his own leg."

Early on in his role as an AEC commissioner, Strauss argued that the United States needed to have a system in place to detect foreign atomic tests. As it turned out, the monitoring system set up at his insistence was established just in time to detect the first Soviet atomic test in August 1949.

The news that the United States no longer had a monopoly on nuclear weapons pitted Strauss against other members of the AEC including its chairman David Lilienthal. Lilienthal wanted to respond to the Soviet test by increasing the production of atomic bombs while at the same time stepping up the effort to create international controls for weapons of mass destruction. Taking a far more aggressive stance, Strauss argued vigorously for a crash program to build a hydrogen bomb: "the time has now come for a quantum jump in our planning . . . . We should now make an intensive effort to get ahead with the super [hydrogen bomb]." Strauss won the day and in January 1950, President Truman publicly announced a "crash" program to build a superbomb.

Conflict over the H-bomb also created tensions between Strauss and physicist J. Robert Oppenheimer, the father of the atomic bomb. Strauss told President Eisenhower that he would only accept the position of AEC chair if Oppenheimer played no role in advising the agency. He explained that he didn't trust Oppenheimer partly because of his consistent opposition to the superbomb. Within days of being sworn into office in July 1953, Strauss had all classified AEC material removed from Oppenheimer's office. By the end of the year, Oppenheimer's security clearance was revoked.

Over the years Strauss's arrogance and his insistence that he was always right made him unpopular on Capitol Hill. In 1959, after two months of exhausting hearings, the Senate rejected his nomination to be Secretary of Commerce. The ordeal was publicly humiliating for Strauss, especially after he was caught lying under oath. Afterward the financier returned permanently to the private sector.

PROLOGUE

Bologna, Italy—September 1928

The bright, late-summer sun beat down on the regal statue of Neptune dominating the Piazza Nettuno in the center of Bologna, Italy, home of the world's oldest university. Neptune seemed to be casting a skeptical eye on the slight, professorial-looking figure in the floppy panama hat and the spade beard sitting at one of the outdoor cafes bordering the square, nursing the last few drops of his afternoon cappuccino. Neither Neptune nor any of the voluble Italians standing in clusters in the square knew that this little man of no apparent consequence staring off into the distance was David Hilbert, probably the most important mathematician of the day. As he finished his coffee and brushed the crumbs of an almond cake off his vest, Hilbert thought once more about the address he would give the next morning to open the International Congress of Mathematicians (ICM) at Bologna University. Hilbert wanted to set the tone of the gathering by focusing the attention of the world's mathematical community on the puzzles he had grappled with for decades and which lay at the very heart of mathematics, puzzles about the logical consistency and completeness of the subject that gives mathematical results the ring of truth found in no other field of intellectual pursuit.

In 1900, at the ICM in Paris that inaugurated the new century, Hilbert, already one of the world's most famous mathematicians, gave an address in which he presented a list of 23 problems that he felt were important for the development of mathematics in the coming century. Now he thought again about the second problem on his list, the one that dealt with the reliability of mathematical reasoning. The mathematical way of getting at the scheme of things—truth or falsity of statements about numbers or other mathematical objects—is deductive. This mode of argumentation begins with a small number of statements taken to be true without benefit of proof, the so-called "axioms" of the logical system used to prove or disprove statements. The rules of logical inference are then used to deduce new true statements—theorems—from the axioms. In his second problem stated at the ICM meeting in 1900, Hilbert wondered whether it was possible to actually *prove* that the axioms themselves were free of contradictions. In other words, given a set of axioms, can it be shown that both a statement and its negation can never be derived by logical deduction from these axioms? If that is the case, the axioms are termed *consistent*. Many years earlier, logicians had shown that if the axioms of a system are inconsistent, *any* statement can be proved. So for a logical system to be useful in separating true from false statements, the bare minimal requirement is that it be consistent.

"Perhaps the Signor would care for another cappuccino?" said the waiter, gliding up to Hilbert's table like an apparition out of the blue. Jerked back to the world of the piazza, Hilbert shook his head and the waiter drifted away as ghostly as he'd arrived. Well, thought Hilbert, I can't sit daydreaming about these matters. I simply must go back to the hotel and go over my notes one more time.

Dropping a few coins on the table for his cappuccino, Hilbert left the cafe and strolled through the lovely arcades surrounding the piazza, reflecting again on the obvious fact that the consistency of a set of axioms is only a special case of the general problem of the provability of any given mathematical statement. Is there a completely mechanical procedure, a kind of mathematical "truth machine" into which any given statement can be inserted, the machine then producing the answer, Yes or No, as to the provability of the statement?

The fast-talking, fast-walking Bolognese who were scurrying through Piazza Nettuno that day could not have guessed that the little man in the strange hat absentmindedly strolling through the piazza was a revolutionary. But by posing the question the next day, Hilbert would throw down a challenge to the mathematical community that would lead to a revolution in our understanding of the limits to human reasoning. Put simply, Hilbert's manifesto would assert that every possible mathematical statement could be settled, true or false. As he put the matter a few years later at his retirement address, "We must know. We will know." But the brilliant Hilbert was wrong! Mathematical reasoning, it turns out, is simply incapable of deciding all statements, even in such a restricted domain of discourse as that of the whole numbers.

Vienna, Austria and Königsberg, Germany—September 1930

The four men sat at a corner table in the Café Reichsrat,

tucked away behind Vienna's City Hall, near the main building of the University of Vienna. The group was talking excitedly and joking among themselves about the upcoming trip to the Second Conference on the Epistemology of the Exact Sciences (EES), which was scheduled to begin in a few days in Königsberg, Germany. The graybeard of the group, 39-year-old logician and philosopher Rudolf Carnap, asked the youngest, 24-year-old Kurt Gödel, about the work he would present at the meeting.

Gödel, slender and shy, looked over at Carnap through thick, round, pebble-style spectacles that gave him the appearance of some type of exotic fish, swimming to look out through the wall of an aquarium. Staring at Carnap, Gödel replied, "I'll present my work on the existence of undecidable propositions in any logical system that's at least as strong as the system used by Russell and Whitehead in *Principia Mathematica*. I've discovered that *every* consistent logical system contains propositions that can be neither proved nor disproved within the framework of that system."

Astonished at what Gödel had just told him, Carnap gasped, "The consequence of this result for Hilbert's program for proving the reliability of mathematics are devastating! You've shown that the entire program outlined by Hilbert was misconceived at the very outset." So, thought Carnap, mathematics is riddled with just as many logical holes and gaps as any other human intellectual undertaking. He smiled to himself as he imagined the shockwaves that would ripple through the philosophical and mathematical community at this result.

"Hilbert will be speaking at the meeting of the Society of German Scientists and Physicians immediately following our meeting," noted Friedrich Waismann, a middle-aged philosopher and member of the celebrated Vienna Circle, a group of philosophers and scientists who met weekly in Vienna to discuss the nature of scientific knowledge. A recent talk there had centered around the logical relationship between mathematics and the natural world. "If Hilbert hears your presentation he's going to explode."

"I don't think Hilbert really has anything new to say about this question of the logical connection between mathematics and nature," chimed in Herbert Feigl, a younger philosopher who also participated in the deliberations of the Vienna Circle. "This is going to be Hilbert's retirement speech, and he's certainly not going to startle the audience with anything new. Königsberg is Hilbert's hometown, and he's going to be made an honorary citizen of the town," noted Feigl. "What kind of revelations can he possibly present, anyway, about nature and logic that he hasn't already made many times before?"

Squinting through the smoky air inside the café at his colleagues as they argued about these fine points of mathematics and nature, Gödel thought how surprised they would all be when they heard the details underlying the bombshell he was planning to drop at the meeting. He still found it hard to believe that the discovery he had made a few months earlier was completely correct, since its implications would undermine the entire program Hilbert had set forth in Bologna a few years earlier for putting the foundations of mathematics on a firm logical basis.

$$\vdots$$

The discussion session on the foundations of mathematics in which Gödel's presentation was scheduled was called to order by the chairman, Professor Hans Hahn, Gödel's teacher at the University of Vienna. Gödel spoke toward the end of the session, criticizing the belief that every statement that can be labeled "true" (or "false") can be represented with certainty in some formal logical system. Gödel then lobbed his bombshell into the discussion, going on to state, "Under the assumption of the consistency of classical mathematics, one can give examples of propositions . . . that are really true, but are unprovable in the formal system of classical mathematics." So the cat was out of the bag—and mathematics would never again be able to claim a degree of truth greater somehow than that claimed by the natural sciences.

Strangely, Gödel's annoucement caused hardly a stir in the audience. Well, the end of a three-day meeting in late summer is hardly the best position on the program to draw anyone's attention. Or perhaps Gödel's claim was just so far away from the conventional wisdom, à la Hilbert, that the audience just didn't *hear* what Gödel was really saying. And, in fact, the written proceedings of the meeting published sometime later did not even mention Gödel. But John von Neumann, newly appointed lecturer at Princeton University, heard Gödel's message loud and clear, and instantly saw the writing on the wall for the demolition of Hilbert's decidability program. Von Neumann buttonholed Gödel immediately after the talk, pressing him for details of the proof for the existence of undecidable propositions. And from that day on, von Neumann knew that his career in mathematical logic had come to a precipitous—but merciful—end.

Cambridge, England—Spring 1935

The short, prematurely bald man strode to the ancient blackboard in the St. John's College lecture hall and began filling it with logical symbols and relations. Turning, Max Newman peered out at the class through his round, wire-framed spectacles and said,

"Here you see one of the big unanswered questions in the foundations of mathematics: Can we find a procedure for deciding the provability of any given proposition? Just recently the Austrian, Kurt Gödel, showed that there must always be some undecidable propositions. But this still leaves open the question of whether there is some single, overarching, systematic procedure for deciding whether any given proposition is or is not decidable. This Decision Problem is the last element of Hilbert's program for the foundations of mathematics that has survived Gödel's onslaught."

As he completed this presentation of Hilbert's *Entscheidungsproblem* (Decision Problem), Newman looked directly at Alan Turing, a shy, dark-haired young man, 15 years his junior, who had already established himself as far and away the sharpest student in the class. The professor thought he would probe Turing just a bit to see how he would react to this puzzle posed by Hilbert.

"How do you think we might go about attacking the Decision Problem, Mr. Turing?"

Plagued by a lifelong hesitancy in speech, a kind of persistent stammer, Turing struggled to formulate his reply. Finally, he gasped out a response to Newman's challenge.

"I believe it would help to consider the steps a human calculator goes through to move from an axiom to the logical statement that either proves or disproves the given proposition."

"Yes," said Newman in his quiet firm manner. "But what do you mean by 'consider the steps'?"

"Well, I'm not exactly sure," stammered Turing. "But something like constructing a systematic procedure (what today we would term an *algorithm*) that represents exactly how a human calculator moves from one configuration of logical symbols, the axioms, to another configuration."

Newman pondered for a moment, then said, "How would such a procedure help you decide whether a particular statement was provable or not?"

"I think you might be able to analyze the algorithm and see if some configurations would be impossible to obtain from the possible starting axioms. If that were the case, you could, in principle, characterize all the undecidable propositions that Gödel showed must exist. But I have to admit that at this moment I don't see clearly how to formulate the informal notion of a 'computation' in precise mathematical terms."

"Perhaps, then, this is an appropriate moment to adjourn for today and contemplate the matter. We'll take up the discussion of this problem next week."

⋮

During the following week, Turing puzzled over the Decision Problem and how he might formally represent the idea of a systematic procedure by which a proposition could be decided. Eventually he came up with the simple idea of a kind of mathematical "machine" whose operation mimicked the steps followed by a human carrying out a computation. Turing's machine (see Figure 1) consists of an infinitely long tape, ruled off into squares, each of which can contain one of a finite number of symbols. It has a reading head that can scan the tape, one square at a time, writing a new symbol on the square or leaving the square unchanged. At any given step the reading head can be in one of a finite number of "states," representing the "state of mind" of the human computer as he or she proceeds through a calculation. Finally, there is a set of instructions (what later came to be called a "program"), which tells the reading head what symbol to print on the current square being scanned, whether to then move one square, left or right, and what state to enter—including the possibility of entering into a stopping state in which the entire process of reading and writing symbols on the tape halts.

In order to decide a given statement, Turing's machine starts with a configuration of symbols on the tape representing one of the axioms of the logical system. From that point on

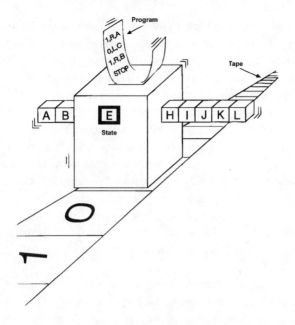

FIGURE 1. A Turing machine.

the machine simply uses the steps in the program to transform the initial configuration into a continuing sequence of new tape configurations, each of which can be interpreted as a theorem that's been proved by the system. So as the machine carries out its program, the initial pattern of symbols on the tape is transformed, step by step, into a sequence of patterns, each corresponding to a theorem proved by the system. In trying to decide if a particular proposition can or cannot be proved by the program, it's only necessary to know if the given configuration will ever arise during the course of following the steps of program as they are carried out by the reading head.

Following Turing's work, researchers saw that it would be important to know if the program will stop after a finite number of steps. If not, it would not be possible ever to know for sure whether the desired configuration will occur. He wondered if there might be some superprogram that could be used to settle this halting problem for any program and any initial tape configuration (axiom) that the program might start with to generate the sequence of patterns on the tape.

Hilbert's belief that there must be a procedure that would decide every proposition had been making the rounds in international mathematical circles since its presentation a few years earlier. One skeptic, G.H. Hardy, was the most famous mathematician in Cambridge. He stated, "There is of course no such theorem, and this is very fortunate, since if there were we should have a mechanical set of rules for the solution of all mathematical problems, and our activities as mathematicians would come to an end." This time the skeptic turned out to be right!

Using his machine, Turing managed to show that the kind of algorithm Hilbert longed for just did not exist. There could not be any systematic way to show that any given program would or would not stop after a finite number of steps when started with a given tape configuration.

Aberdeen, Maryland—August 1944

Late again, thought Herman Goldstine, as he paced the railway platform on a sweltering late-summer afternoon in Aberdeen, wondering just how late the train to Philadelphia was going to be today. A slightly built, bespectacled new lieutenant in the U.S. Army, the 31-year-old Goldstine had been stationed at the Aberdeen Proving Ground two years earlier where he employed his mathematical talents to help discover why the proto-computer known as the Electronic Numerical Integrator and Computer (ENIAC), being built at the University of Pennsylvania's Moore School of Electrical Engineering in nearby Philadelphia, was not working as well as expected. And since the army had a substantial investment in this machine, which they hoped to use for various computational tasks involving the calculation of ballistic trajectories, the military brass thought that Goldstine's presence in Philadelphia might not only beef up the mathematical talent on hand for the job but also inject a bit of military zip into the slack work attitudes that military men always seem to find in academics.

Upon reaching one end of the platform, Goldstine turned and began to retrace his steps, his head down, deep in reflection on the discussions that day at the Proving Grounds. A noise at the other end of the platform broke into his reverie, and as he glanced up he saw a rather portly figure in a gray, three-piece banker's suit come onto the platform and begin walking in his direction. Goldstine was startled when he recognized this fellow traveler as the legendary mathematician John von Neumann. He must be on his way to Philadelphia to catch the train back to Princeton, thought Goldstine. Besides the two of them, the platform was deserted. Goldstine wondered if fate had conspired to place von Neumann here at this very moment, since the mathematical problem he had been discussing just an hour ago with his colleagues J. Presper Eckert and John W. Mauchly at the Moore School was the very one he had often wanted to speak to von Neumann about. Goldstine was also curious about the atmosphere at von Neumann's home institution, the prestigious Institute for Advanced Study in Princeton. Following his graduate work in mathematics in Chicago, Goldstine had been offered a position there as assistant to one of the Institute's other world-famous mathematicians, Marston Morse, before the army stepped in to commandeer his services for the war effort. I'll never have a better opportunity to speak to von Neumann than now, thought Goldstine. So he nervously approached the great man.

"Excuse me, sir, but aren't you Professor von Neumann?" asked Goldstine in a timid voice.

"I am," replied von Neumann with a questioning look. "May I ask who you are, Lieutenant? Have we met before?"

"Not at all. But I have heard you lecture several times, and wanted to take this opportunity to introduce myself. I am Herman Goldstine. Currently, I'm stationed here at the Aberdeen Proving Grounds."

"I see," said von Neumann in his soft Hungarian-accented English, which, together with his warm, friendly personality, always seemed to put people at ease. "Are you doing mathematical work here?"

"Actually, I received my doctoral degree in mathematics at Chicago a couple of years ago and was offered a post at the Institute as assistant to your colleague, Professor Morse. But the army needed me more than the Institute. So here I am."

"Are you at liberty to say what you're working on here?" enquired von Neumann.

"In general terms, yes. I'm here to help develop a computing machine that the army is supporting. It's actually being built at the Moore School down at Penn. But I'm stationed here at Aberdeen, because the army wants to use this machine to calculate various sorts of ballistic trajectories."

Hearing this, von Neumann's expression changed from a half-attentive, cocktail-party type of look to a gaze of intense concentration. "Did you say you're involved in building a computing machine?"

"Yes, it's going to be based on electronic circuitry using vacuum tubes—if we can ever get it going. A big part of my job here is to put a bit of military discipline into the situation at Penn, so as to move this project forward a bit faster."

"What type of performance do you expect to get from this machine?" von Neumann shot back, his tone now more typical of an oral examination for a doctoral candidate than the relaxed good humor of a casual conversation.

"Well, the design specs call for the machine to be able to

carry out 333 multiplications per second."

As he heard this astonishing figure, von Neumann's eyebrows shot up. As the train approached the station, he said,

"Young man, please sit with me on the train and tell me as much about this project as security considerations allow."

⋮

And so began von Neumann's association as a consultant to the ENIAC Project and its successor, the Electronic Discrete Variable Computer (EDVAC). Both machines were being developed by the brilliant electrical engineer, J. Presper Eckert, along with his somewhat less dynamic colleague, John W. Mauchly. At the time von Neumann joined the project, the principal flaw of the ENIAC was its lack of adequate stored memory. Every time the machine was to tackle a new problem, cables had to be rerouted, dials changed, and switches set in new positions to specify the new problem. Von Neumann, following the work of Eckert, hit upon the idea of storing the machine's program in memory in coded form rather than specifying it by hardware. And so returned the idea, probably first enunciated by Charles Babbage a century earlier, of *software* dictating the course of a calculation, hardware serving only as a kind of material embodiment of the information being processed by the machine.

At this point von Neumann, with his characteristic flair for jumping several steps ahead of mere ordinary geniuses, was already seeing relations between the computing machine and the human brain, and beginning to think about how he might have a real-life computing machine of his own. And therein lies our tale.

Chapter One

A WALK DOWN MERCER STREET

The tall, heavyset man strolling slowly down the sidewalk was dressed in the rumpled, dark-blue sweatshirt, baggy pants, and unshined shoes—with no socks —of the typical absent-minded professor. Glancing up, he saw a small boy on a bicycle bearing down on him, and had to quickly step aside, his long, white hair flying, as the boy nearly crashed into him, doing a comic double take as he caught a passing glimpse of one of the world's best-known faces. With the famous droopy gray mustache, dark, soulful eyes, and a large, heavily built body yielding to the ravages of age, the man looked more like a retired football player or an aging wrestler than the most publicly celebrated scientist since Isaac Newton. If face and name recognition were any measure to judge by, the man might well rank higher than the President or the

Pope. Yet in the small, intensely academic town of Princeton, New Jersey, Albert Einstein, the most distinguished professor at the famed Institute for Advanced Study (IAS), was just one more senior citizen dodging young mothers with strollers—and children on bicycles—on his daily walk from the Institute to his home on Mercer Street on this rather warm, early-spring afternoon.

The diminutive figure at Einstein's side could not have presented a sharper physical contrast to the great man. He was gaunt to the point of emaciation and a black streak running through the middle of of his thinning, gray hair plastered back in the fashion of a Roaring Twenties matinee idol gave the top of his head an astonishing resemblance to a skunk. As the pair strolled side by side, the small man struggled with a bulging briefcase that appeared to weigh almost as much as himself, making him appear more like Einstein's lawyer than the greatest logician since Aristotle, which is how many of his peers described Kurt Gödel. He wore a thick, black scarf wound tightly about his neck and was bundled up in a winter-weight tweed suit, woolen vest, and old-fashioned necktie. Even in the moderately warm spring weather, Gödel's hypochondria knew no bounds and dictated that he protect himself against the ever-present threat of disease from germs and other pathogens that only he seemed to sense.

Deep in his thoughts, Gödel paused for a moment and peered up at Einstein through a pair of perfectly round, dark-rimmed, thick spectacles of the type usually seen only on wartime refugees from central Europe. Stepping off the sidewalk, Einstein paused to allow a car to pass. Looking over at his companion, he noticed Gödel's hunched shoulders and deep worry lines, which prompted him to enquire, "What is troubling you, Kurt? You have been silent for too long now. Is something on your mind?"

Peering up at Einstein with a soulful, almost hangdog

look on his face, Gödel replied: "I'm sorry, Albert. I don't really want to bother you with my small problems," the corners of his mouth turning up in a shy, embarrassed smile.

"You are beginning to irritate me, Kurt. We are friends for a long time, no? What are friends for if not to help each other? Now tell me, what is bothering you."

Gödel stared off into space, his mind seemingly transported to one of those ethereal realms beyond space and time that only logicians can access. A passerby would have found it comical indeed to see these two giants of the intellect, in a state of seemingly complete paralysis on the sidewalks of Princeton, totally absorbed in thought. Breaking out of his reverie, Gödel finally blurted out what was bothering him. He began with a question:

"Do you remember when I first came to the Institute?"

"Yes. It was in its first year of operation, 1933. Am I right?"

Gödel nodded and went on to tell Einstein that he had regularly shuttled back and forth between Vienna and Princeton from that initial visit until he finally left Nazi-occupied Vienna for the last time in January 1940. He moved permanently to Princeton following a tortuous journey by rail across Siberia, by ship to San Francisco, and then across the United States by train to New Jersey. This roundabout itinerary had been necessary to avoid a dangerous crossing of the U-boat-infested North Atlantic.

Passing beneath the branches of a majestic oak tree whose leaves were just starting to open, Gödel asked, "By offering me these many visiting appointments, do you think the Institute authorities have demonstrated their recognition of my work and its importance in the world of mathematics?"

"Definitely, Kurt. No question about that," replied Einstein, wondering just where Gödel was going with these questions.

"Then why have I not been appointed Professor in the faculty of the School of Mathematics? Certainly all the professors—Veblen, Alexander, Morse, von Neumann, Weyl—fully deserve their positions. I can find no logical argument against any of them being Professor. But I am still a 'Member' of the Institute, not a Professor on the faculty. I find this very puzzling and, to be bluntly honest, personally and professionally insulting."

Finally, the matter was in the open. Gödel was upset because he had not been appointed a full professor at the Institute. Despite his being universally acclaimed as the greatest logician of the twentieth century, some even calling him the greatest logician since Aristotle, the faculty of the IAS had in its strange brand of wisdom relegated Gödel to the lower rank of Member of the Institute, albeit for life, but not Professor.

Before Einstein could reply, Gödel's unnatural fear of and inborn respect for authority percolated to the surface of his consciousness and, in some agitation, he declared: "Of course, maybe the Institute management has a good reason for not promoting me to Professor. Perhaps there is some question of my loyalty to the United States, or someone has questioned the ultimate value of my work. Do you think that could be the case?"

Taken completely aback at this plaintive, almost paranoiac, statement, Einstein was momentarily speechless. As a man who had been lionized by the entire world for decades, he just didn't know what to say or how to soothe Gödel's wounded ego and defuse what could easily blow up into a real conflict in upcoming faculty meetings. Like a kindly Dutch uncle, he put his hand on Gödel's shoulder and said softly, "Kurt, the entire faculty understands the importance of your work. Professor von Neumann even asked once how any of us could consider ourselves 'Professor' if you are not. Your results in mathematics and logic will live as long as men do mathematics and logic. They are the epitome of what the IAS is about: abstract thought that uncovers the deepest secrets of nature and the human mind."

By this statement Einstein acknowledged that in an institute in which abstract theory was the coin of the realm, Gödel was the unchallenged Grand Exalted Ruler. His stunning discovery of the limitations of all axiomatic deductive systems of logic placed him—and his work—in a separate category from the normal run of academic geniuses. In the one, true, platonic heaven of the IAS, Gödel was King. Einstein's tribute led to the inevitable rejoinder: "Then it's only logical for me to wonder why, if the faculty holds my work in such high esteem, they have not voted to promote me to Professor. Do you have an answer for that?"

Einstein knew he would be painted into a corner if he responded in any fashion at all and desperately wished that he had walked home alone. He had to say something. Yet getting into a logical debate with Gödel was about as much fun as wrestling with an alligator—and just about as painful. Running his hand through his electrified hair, Einstein said softly, but firmly, "Kurt, von Neumann has argued the case for your promotion in the faculty meetings. I have, too. But there are always some faculty members who vote against it. The strange thing is that they don't offer any arguments against your promotion that can really be logically analyzed. Instead they fall back on statements about how important it is to give you ample time for your research and not to distract you from it with mundane administrative chores like committee meetings, evaluating applicants for visiting positions, and the appointment of new faculty. Yes, it is very difficult to argue against such beliefs."

"I understand the situation and I am grateful for your support. But perhaps you could have a short talk with Oppenheimer or someone else in the administration about this for me? You are the most influential member of the faculty, and perhaps a word from you to Oppenheimer could change the faculty's mind."

Einstein sighed. "Unfortunately, you overrate my influence. When I came to the Institute in 1933, Mr. Flexner [founder and first director of the IAS] made it perfectly clear by his actions that he had bought me for the Institute and that my role here was to be a ceremonial figurehead, an icon, if you like. Now I am afraid the faculty thinks of me as a bit of a dinosaur. They tolerate my ideas more from respect for my past work than from enthusiasm for my current ideas, especially my very unfashionable views on quantum theory. So I don't think my speaking with Oppenheimer is going to help your cause at all, my friend. Nevertheless, I promise you I will try."

⋮

Glancing up at the watery sunlight streaming down from behind a fleecy cloud, Einstein was pleased to see the weather clearing. Perhaps he could even sit for a while in his garden this afternoon and take a bit of sun before the wind came up again. This benevolent turn of nature put him into an optimistic frame of mind as he declared, "Enough of petty academic politics, Kurt. Let us talk a bit about something of substance and content. What are you working on these days?"

"Your own general theory of relativity," announced Gödel with a sly grin, surprising the great physicist. And within the blink of an eye the two were discussing Einstein's most stunning achievement, the general theory of relativity, perhaps the greatest single piece of work in the history of physics. In essence, the general theory of relativity is a theory of gravity, and soon the pair were deep in consideration of one of the theory's most startling implications about our everyday sense of the flow of time.

In his high-pitched, sing-song voice, Gödel said that as part of an essay he was preparing for a book honoring Einstein's scientific and philosophical work, he had been studying the mathematical equations underpinning the theory. These equations admit different solutions, each solution leading to a very different type of universe—some with space twisted like a pretzel, others with time moving in ways counter to everyday human intuition. One universe is expanding, another contracting, while in yet another, space and time are so strongly curved that it is possible to literally look back into one's own past. But the startling new solution Gödel had discovered involved a universe in which there is no objective lapse of time at all. So in Gödel's universe the ideas of "before" and "after" had no intrinsic meaning. One person's "before" could be another's "after," and vice versa. Gödel was concerned about whether such a *mathematical* universe could be taken seriously as a candidate for the actual physical universe we inhabit.

Looking over at Einstein to see how he was taking these strange notions, Gödel nearly ran head on into a housewife pulling a grocery cart down Mercer Street on her way back from the market. The woman stared in momentary puzzlement at the great Einstein, who looked vaguely familiar to her. But as he had the young cyclist earlier, Einstein ignored the woman and encouraged Gödel to elaborate.

"I have recently discovered a remarkable solution to the field equations of general relativity," Gödel declared excitedly. "My solution implies the possibility of traveling backward in time. If this mathematical universe that I have derived—from your own theory, mind you—describes the universe we live in, then I can see no alternative to a complete denial of the reality of time; it is simply an illusion, a trick of the mind with no basis in physical reality at all."

Stopped in his tracks by this remarkable claim, Einstein

stared at Gödel for at least a minute before saying, "Please, slow down and go through your argument carefully for me. Give me a clear explanation of the reasoning that could lead you to such an amazing statement."

Robin redbreasts twittered in the trees, cars passed on the street, clouds moved in front of the sun. Everyday life went on all around. But Gödel was oblivious to all these everyday things, as he stood, fixed in place on the street corner, biting his lip and furrowing his brow, marshalling his arguments. He wanted to be clear, but . . . .

"First, think about your own *special* theory of relativity. In that theory the notion of 'now' is not the same for every observer. What is 'now' and what is 'before' and 'after' depends entirely on what point of reference an observer uses to measure spatial and temporal events. Different frames of reference give different moments for what constitutes 'now.' "

"That is certainly the case," Einstein agreed, thinking of the now famous Twin Paradox. This involves identical twins, one of whom travels at a speed close to that of light on a space ship to the outer reaches of the galaxy, while the other twin stays at home. When the traveling twin returns, he discovers to his great surprise that his brother has aged several decades—or even centuries—*relative* to his own age. This so-called "paradox" is simply a manifestation of the fact that time does not move at the same rate for everyone. The closer to the speed of light you move, the slower your clock runs relative to the clock of a stationary observer like the stay-at-home twin.

"But the relativity of this kind of *intuitive* time implies the relativity of an objective span of time that would be the same for all observers. Such an objective interval of time, in turn, implies that only the present really exists. But this is impossible."

Grasping Gödel's point immediately, Einstein finished the

argument.

"So if the *special* theory of relativity is true, *time disappears* completely. No?"

"Precisely," agreed Gödel.

Einstein thought for a moment, his sad brown eyes staring off into that same distant realm Gödel had looked into earlier, a place reserved for those few geniuses gifted with the ability to see beyond ordinary space and time. Jerking his thoughts back from distant galaxies and possible universes to the plain, simple streets of Princeton, he finally said, "But such a conclusion is very much confined to the particular—and nonphysical— situation in which there are no preferred frames of reference, a situation in which every observer is just as good as any other observer. This is the domain of the *special* theory of relativity. But in the *general* theory of relativity some reference frames are privileged. These privileged frames can be coordinated with each other to determine a single, objective, cosmic time. So in our universe *time reappears.* Doesn't that destroy your argument for whatever real universe we happen to inhabit?"

"Not at all," said Gödel, his voice rising again in the peculiar high-pitched giggle he fell into when especially excited. "My new solution of the equations of general relativity yields a set of world models that *rotate.* I can prove that in such worlds *cosmic time disappears.* Moreover, in certain nonexpanding universes of this type, there are even closed timelike world lines, paths for an individual's movement through space and time in the four-dimensional realm of *spacetime,* that return to exactly where they began."

Almost as if he were afraid to speak the words, Einstein muttered more to himself than to Gödel, "You mean time travel?"

"Yes, time travel!" Gödel smiled. "But if you can revisit the past, it never passed from existence in the first place. So once again, *time disappears.*"

"But, Kurt," Einstein countered, "your new rotating universe is merely a possible world, one that comes out of the mathematics but might not correspond to any type of physical reality."

Gödel, however, was ready for this fairly straightforward objection. "The only way our universe and a rotating universe can differ is in the global distribution of matter and in the motions of the two universes. The real universe and the mathematical one are described by the same laws of nature, and it's certainly conceivable that they could give observers the same experiences of time. So if time is an illusion in one world, it must be an illusion in the other one, too."

Einstein nodded his approval of this airtight chain of logical deduction. Time indeed seemed to stop for Einstein as he again retreated into his own inner world, contemplating the implications of Gödel's result: Time would indeed *disappear* even in the actual world.

Breaking out of his trance, Einstein suggested, "Perhaps we could learn more about the nature of your rotating world by examining more closely the nature of the time travel it admits. What *kind* of time travel is it? Backward in time, forward, both, or . . . ?"

"Yes," said Gödel rather diffidently. "In the universe determined by my solution, travel into the future or the past is possible in exactly the same way we can travel in different directions in space."

Einstein enquired calmly, "So there is no distinction between 'earlier' and 'later'?"

Gödel's face lit up in a grin that would do justice to a Cheshire cat, as he replied: "Exactly. What I am now puzzling over is whether there is any type of measurement that can be taken in our universe that would exclude such a time-travel universe as a candidate for the universe we actually inhabit. I must study this matter very carefully."

"Kurt, my friend, you get closer and closer to becoming a physicist with each passing day," joked Einstein, his saintly face breaking into a smile.

"You know, I began my university studies in theoretical physics before being seduced by the logical purity of mathematics. But to be truthful, my interests are now leaning more and more toward the philosophical, not the physical or even the logical."

"These ideas on the illusory nature of time certainly seem far more philosophical than real to me," Einstein agreed dryly. "I admire the logical clarity and precision of your argument. But I am still convinced that your mathematical universe is not our universe. God is subtle—but he is not malicious enough to play such a lowly trick on us poor mortals as to give us the possibility of time travel."

Gödel thought about his friend's comment as the pair continued their walk in silence. A few minutes later Einstein observed, "You know, Kurt, this time-travel result is very similar in spirit to your earlier work on incompleteness in mathematics. You realize that, no?"

Gödel looked as if he'd been struck by lightning. "What do you mean?" he cried. "We're talking about a physical situation here, not a logical structure like arithmetic."

"Yes," said Einstein, "but your own Incompleteness Theorem uses the formal argumentation of mathematical logic to prove that it is impossible to define the 'intuitive' concept of Truth within any logical framework. Now you have again used mathematical methods to show that relativity theory cannot capture the 'intuitive' concept of time."

Gödel nodded in agreement with Einstein's analogy. As Gödel pondered, Einstein continued. "But what is strange to me is that in the case of truth, you conclude that the limitation lies within formalized mathematics. Yet in the situation of time, you do not say that the limitation is with relativity theory, but that intuitive time itself is an illusion. You know, Kurt, you are coming very close to violating the logician's first rule of life—consistency," joked Einstein, to Gödel's evident consternation.

⋮

While Einstein intended his little joke to relax Gödel and show that he understood that there were both serious logical and physical puzzles to be solved in coming to terms with these two great discoveries, the subtext of the joke underscored the common methodological components forming the basis of Gödel's two stunning foundational results in mathematics and in cosmology. The first is the use of mathematical argumentation to probe the limits of formal mathematics in capturing intuitive concepts—truth in arithmetic, time in the physical universe. The second aspect is the wish to move from the possible to the actual. Gödel believed that in certain situations what is possible tells us about what is, in fact, actual. In this latter case, his reflections on the mere *possibility* of a "Gödel Universe," in which time is nonexistent, leads him to conclude that time does not exist in the *actual* world.

Gödel's Incompleteness Theorem of mathematics and Einstein's Special Theory of Relativity, along with that other foundational result of twentieth-century science, Heisenberg's Uncertainty Principle, share considerable common ground. The first challenges the idea that every mathematical proposition can be proved or disproved by logical deduction, while the second demolishes the notion of a "cosmic clock" beating out a sequence of time moments valid for all observers. Finally, Heisenberg's result shows the logical, not just the practical, limits to the accuracy with which we can measure the physical properties of objects, properties such as their position and velocity or time and energy. Not only does each of these results represent one of the great theoretical achievements of the twentieth century, but each also has deep philosophical implications for how we humans see the world. Specifically, each result is established by formal mathematical methods, while demonstrating in its own way a type of *limitation* in the relevant area of enquiry—arithmetic and physics. Gödel shows an inherent limitation within any consistent framework of logical deduction, Einstein says there is a limit to the speed of light, and Heisenberg sets a limit on our ability to simultaneously measure different properties of a fundamental particle. Finally, all three draw conclusions about the way *the world is* from what are basically assumptions about the nature of knowledge, epistemological assumptions. So, in essence, they each argue that there are *limits* to what we can know about the world around us by using the tools of logical analysis and mathematics.

As the pair reached Einstein's white clapboard house, a surprisingly modest dwelling for the century's most famous scientist, the great physicist patted Gödel on the shoulder, turned into his walkway, and bade him farewell. As they parted, Einstein encouraged Gödel to develop further those strange ideas about the nature of time. Walking up the front steps and onto his porch, he turned and watched as Gödel slowly trudged down Mercer Street toward his own home. How odd, thought Einstein. The wizened little man bundled up in the heavy overcoat is one of the greatest intellects of the century. Yet no one really knows him—not even his own colleagues on the Institute faculty. Perhaps *der Herr Gott* really is malicious, after all.

Chapter Two

TEATIME AT THE IAS

Three o'clock in the afternoon: teatime in the Institute's Commons Room, a warm, wood-paneled room conjuring an image of cigars and brandy in the library of an English country manor instead of an American academic research center. Teatime was an honored tradition at the IAS that everyone respected, no matter how busy or engaged in their work. The Commons Room was the waterhole of intellectual life, where faculty, visitors, and hangers-on all met on an equal footing to discuss and argue the issues of the day.

On this particular afternoon, the legendary poet, T.S. Eliot, sat in the overstuffed leather chair in the corner reading last week's London *Times*. As he hid behind the paper, peering intently through rounder-than-round librarian's spectacles, the pale, graying, emaciated-looking Eliot eagerly digested the literary news from across the Atlantic. A poet adrift in a sea of mathematicians and physicists, Eliot wondered why he had ever given in to the blandishments of IAS Director J. Robert Oppenheimer to "spend a term in Princeton." Where is the poetry in the concept of an electron buzzing around the atomic nucleus or in the equations of an operator algebra? Where is the rhyme or the rhythm or the meter in the symbols making up the gauge theories of particle physics? He felt as out of place there as a dustman at the King's garden party.

Near the tea table against the wall, deeply engaged in what was really an intense debate masquerading as polite tea-time conversation, stood the German mathematician, physicist, and general polymath, Hermann Weyl (pronounced "vile") and the energetic Viennese theoretical physicist, Wolfgang Pauli. The two were a study in contrasts. Weyl, with hair as gray as his bland, three-piece suit, gold-rimmed pedant's glasses, and dark, tightly knotted tie spotted conservatively with white polka dots, reminded Eliot of a distant uncle or, perhaps, a type of banker Eliot had dealt with in his previous life as a banker himself, the type who can't quite bring himself to ignore an overdraft. Pauli, outspoken and ebullient, was a short, stout, dark-haired, and often dark-tempered, antagonist. The long-term visitor from the Eidgenössische Technische Hochschule (ETH) in Zurich was certainly the sharpest critic in the entire theoretical physics community. Even Oppenheimer, no mean critic himself, had to take a back seat in the seminar room when the acerbic Austrian rose to render a judgment on some gap in an argument or a poorly presented idea. In 1945 Pauli had been awarded the Nobel Prize in physics for his work on the so-called "Pauli Exclusion Principle," which states that no two quantum objects—two electrons, for instance—can occupy the same physical state at the same time. This result, which Pauli discovered in 1928, was central to the development of both particle and quantum physics, since it provided a physical constraint that helped researchers sort through and eliminate many mathematically appealing, but physically unrealizable, theories of matter and energy.

Unlike the nearly somnolent Eliot, the two emigrés from Nazi tyranny rattled their teacups and waved their biscuits about with abandon, as they threw off waves of intellectual energy in a staccato-like German, arguing the difference, if any, between the type of knowledge that mathematicians recognize and that which is acknowledged by natural scientists, in particular, particle physicists like Pauli.

"In mathematics," argued Weyl vehemently, his faint German accent still noticeable, "we have the notion of proof. This gives us a clear-cut, unambiguous way to create new knowledge from old. We start with the old knowledge—the axioms of a logical system—and employ the tools of deductive inference to generate new true statements—theorems—from the old ones."

Pauli glowered at the simplistic nature of this mathematician's view of the world, sputtering, "The problem with this approach is that there is no criterion by which you can claim the initial knowledge, the axioms, are really knowledge. They may or may not accord with our sense of the world and the way things are. You state the axiom that two parallel lines intersect at infinity, even though in the real world there are no such infinities and parallel lines never meet. But this obvious fact is irrelevant for mathematicians. They care only about logical consistency. No physicist would ever accept a hypothesis that runs counter to observation or laboratory measurement."

The patrician Weyl was not at all put off by this outburst. He'd heard it all many times before. "Of course, of course," he replied, in a good-natured attempt to calm Pauli down, speaking as if to an excited child. "The situation is really a bit worse than this, even in mathematics. We have no clear consensus about what kinds of logical operations can be used in creating new knowledge."

Eliot's poetic soul cringed at this interchange, which he was following from a distance with increasing interest. The views of both Pauli and Weyl on what constituted "knowledge" certainly did not accord with the intuitive idea of knowledge that any poet, humanist, or artist would almost certainly endorse. Weyl appeared to be saying that mathematical knowledge could come only from following a set of rules by which one logically deduces a conclusion from a set of more or less arbitrary assumptions. As for Pauli, the physicist, his view of knowledge as something that can be measured was hardly much better. What a severely stunted notion of knowledge these men and their fields have! thought Eliot. Perhaps Oppenheimer brought me here to try to add a bit of scope and breadth of humanistic vision to these deliberations. It's a pity the chasm between the scientist and the poet is as wide as the Grand Canyon—and even harder to bridge. The very possibility of a meaningful dialogue between poetry and science seems hopelessly remote, he thought sadly.

Eliot's musings echoed perfectly the thoughts on the poetry/science divide expressed by another regular visitor to the Institute, British physicist Paul Dirac, also a Nobel laureate, honored in 1933 for his mathematical work predicting the existence of anti-particles like the positron, which have the same mass as their ordinary matter counterparts but with an opposite electrical charge and magnetic moment (spin). Such objects were later observed in actual experiments. Dirac once expressed puzzlement over Oppenheimer's predilection for writing poetry and studying Latin, asking him seriously, "How can you do both—poetry and physics? In physics we try to tell people things in such a way that they understand something that nobody knew before. In the case of poetry it's the exact opposite. There one takes something that everyone knows and tries to express it in ways that nobody ever saw before."

Suddenly a cacophony of voices sounded from the hall outside the Commons Room doorway as a new group of faculty, postdoctoral students, and visitors bustled into the room. As they clustered around the tea table, pouring as much tea on the tablecloth as into their cups and quickly grabbing for the few biscuits remaining, everyone turned to the commanding figure at the center of the crowd, former head of the Manhattan Project to build the atomic bomb and now Director of the IAS, J. Robert Oppenheimer, known to one and all as "Oppie." Charismatic in the way of a religious ascetic or mystic, yet dressed in an impeccable three-piece, gray business suit more commonly seen on diplomats or politicians than on academics, Oppenheimer had the gaunt, cadaverous look of someone who slept very little and smoked far too much. Yet a look from his razor-sharp, intensely blue eyes could cause even the most egomaniacal of the Institute's supercharged intellects to stop in their tracks and pay attention when Oppenheimer spoke. In short, he had the type of "star quality" that one can only be born with but can never acquire.

Picking up on the conversation between Weyl and Pauli, Oppenheimer turned to Eliot and asked in a resonant directorial voice, "Well, Tom, I see that Pauli and Weyl haven't yet managed to reconcile themselves in the realm of physics. What do you think about the aesthetic differences between the poet and the physicist?" But before the shy, retiring Eliot could overcome his surprise at being asked directly about this question and frame a reply, Oppenheimer went on, saying to the group, "There's a very big difference between the knowledge a poet expresses in a sonnet about love and the knowledge a neurochemist would acquire if he measured the concentration of chemicals in the brain when his patient is told to think about his loved one. What Pauli is talking about is *scientific* knowledge; what a genius like Eliot here means by knowledge is an entirely different thing."

Such was the majesty of Oppenheimer's tone and bearing as he made this pronouncement that everyone in the room was struck silent. After all, who could argue with him on a matter of philosophy? Or poetry? Or physics? Finally, Oppenheimer's former teacher, Pauli, broke the spell by questioning the distinction he had just drawn.

"How can you say that? How are you able to distinguish between the knowledge we have of the mass of an electron and what Eliot would call knowledge of a loved one or the shape and color of a rose?"

"There is something I would call 'soul,'" said Oppenheimer in a strong voice that carried conviction. "Or what some mystics and practitioners of Eastern religions term The One. Here is where poets and artists draw their knowledge from, not from looking at a photograph showing the trace of an elementary particle in a cyclotron or measuring the charge of a proton in a cloud chamber. Platonists, like our colleague Gödel, would call The One by the everyday label 'intuition' or 'feel.' Whatever you call it, though, it's every bit as real and means every bit as much as the knowledge we physicists take to be the 'true facts' of Nature." Finishing his pronouncement, Oppenheimer picked up his teacup, symbolically opening the floor for discussion.

⋮

The question was a very old and venerable one. Philosophers call it epistemology, which addresses the issues, What is knowledge? How do we obtain it? How can we verify it? What are its limits? What is the relationship between what is known and the person who knows it?

The simplest and most traditional answer to the question, "What constitutes knowledge?" is that it is true, justified belief. Regrettably, this commonsense, almost flip, reply creates more questions than it answers, and is certainly open to debate about what is *true*. What is a *belief?* What do we mean by *justified* belief? The linguistic philosopher, Ludwig Wittgenstein, for instance, would say that knowledge is simply the by-product of a particular worldview rather than being some objective thing that just sits "out there" waiting for us to discover it.

The physicists engaged in this teatime Princetonian debate had also drawn attention to whether science or mathematics has a privileged position insofar as creation of knowledge goes. Is there something intrinsically different—perhaps superior, even—in the type of knowledge we create in either of these areas? In fact, what do we even mean by "mathematical knowledge" or "scientific knowledge"?

Taking advantage of Oppenheimer's momentary withdrawal to the sidelines, one of the younger mathematicians visiting the Institute for a term entered the fray. The frail-looking young man had the stooped appearance of someone who spent too much time with books and not enough in the fresh air. Speaking in a high-pitched, strangely schoolboyish voice heavy with the accent of his native France, he pushed his lanky blond hair off his forehead before remarking that the idea of truth used in mathematics and the very same concept as understood in everyday terms are completely different. He noted that Gödel's stunning results showed that there is an eternally unbridegable gap between the two. As he stated to the teatime group: "Everyday 'truth' is always a bigger concept than the mathematician's truth."

Wishing he could recall the name of this bright French visitor (was it Weil or Cartan?), Oppenheimer glanced over at Weyl and raised his eyebrows as if to say, "This young fellow has thrown the ball back into your court, my friend," since he knew perfectly well that Weyl was a strong critic of the implications of Gödel's results for mathematics. This was especially true for the type of interpretation that accepted the Law of the

Excluded Middle, by which a mathematical proposition could be only true or false, provable or unprovable. An intuitionist, like Weyl, could never accept the idea of proving something true by proving that it is not false. And his reply to the young mathematician did not disappoint.

"Gödel's discovery places a constant drain on the enthusiasm with which I pursue my scientific work," Weyl stated rather sadly, glancing up at the ceiling as if hoping for heavenly deliverance from the plague that Gödel had visited upon his view of mathematical truth.

"In what way?" asked Pauli, trying to draw out Weyl on a matter that Weyl was clearly uncomfortable in discussing.

"Scientists and mathematicians are not indifferent to what their work means in the context of human caring, suffering, and creative existence in the world. But Gödel's results prevent us from gaining a full understanding of the cosmos as a necessary truth," Weyl said by way of explanation.

"Are you saying that the only real way to prove something is true is to actually construct it from the natural numbers 1, 2, 3, . . . ?" asked one of the physicists in the room.

"Yes," Weyl stated with some intensity. "Nonconstructive existence proofs, which show that something exists by proving its nonexistence is false, is like informing the world that a treasure exists without disclosing its location. Mathematics should be much more definite than this about the objects it studies."

Oppenheimer was not ready to settle for this kind of defeatist attitude toward Gödel's incompleteness results, and asked Weyl if he thought Gödel's work robbed him of his reason for being a scientist.

"It seems that on the strength of Gödel's Theorem, the ultimate foundations of the constructions of mathematical physics will remain trapped forever in a level of thinking involving analogies and intuitions. This implies that there are limits to the precision of certainty, that even in theoretical physics there is a boundary."

"And where is this boundary residing?" Pauli asked forcefully.

"The boundary is the scientist himself, as a thinker," shot back Weyl with equal force.

"This seems a rather self-focused, almost solipsist view of what we can know, even in science," interjected Oppenheimer, "although it's not very far away from what quantum theorists seem to believe when they speak about the process of observation *creating* properties such as the spin and position of objects like electrons."

Weyl set his teacup down on a sidetable and gazed out to the woods beyond the window, pondering what could be known in mathematics and how it contrasts with what these physicists were claiming about physical reality. Does the world of natural science contain the very same kind of limits on what can be known that Gödel showed must necessarily exist in mathematics? And what about Gödel's results themselves?

Eliot had finally heard enough and simply had to jump into this debate. In a soft, almost deferential manner, he stated, "I always had the idea that scientists did calculations as a way of getting at the scheme of things. Is it not possible that the theories of matter, the universe, energy, and so forth could be thought of as prescriptions for calculating and predicting something? Couldn't these predictions then be tested in laboratory experiments to validate or refute the predictions?"

Before any of the others could open their mouths to even begin to reply, Oppenheimer's lightning-fast mind had already formulated a fully developed position on Eliot's query. In fact, the reply came so fast that it seemed almost as if he and Eliot had been in telepathic communion on the matter.

"What Eliot asks is whether all that we can hope to know about the world 'as it is' is what we can read on a measuring instrument. That instrument might be a meter stick, the dial of a voltmeter, the track on a photographic plate, or even the sensory response of the human nervous system. 'Instrumentalism' is what some philosophers of science call this view of the world. But I think there is more to knowledge than just reading the position of a needle on a dial. I'm sure you agree, Pauli?"

"Yes, most definitely," concurred the Viennese quickly. "There is more poetry in physics than in a meter stick or a particle accelerator. Measurements tell us *about* reality; they are not reality itself. Physics and other sciences, in general, try to understand deep reality. They are not just theories of measurement and numerology."

At this pronouncement from the highest of high priests of theoretical science, one of the visitors to the physics group muttered *soto voce* that such a view was fine for a philosopher, but that Eliot was right: scientific knowledge was about the consequences of following rules, formulas, and prescriptions, and thus differed considerably from the kind of general knowledge that IAS brahmins Oppenheimer, Pauli, and Weyl were espousing. What a pity that John von Neumann was not present for this discussion. The only mind at the IAS as fast as Oppenheimer's might have shed a very different light on the matter. Perhaps scientific knowledge, à la von Neumann, will be on tomorrow's teatime agenda, hoped the visitor.

⋮

The plate of biscuits having been reduced to a pile of crumbs and the teapot nearly drained, teatime was clearly over. As the group disbanded and began drifting out of the room and back to their offices, Weyl whispered to Oppenheimer that he'd like a quick word. As Eliot showed no signs of either vacating his armchair or abandoning his newspaper, the pair moved to the corner of the Commons Room for a bit of privacy.

In a low voice, Weyl began, "You know, Robert, I am very concerned about Johnny's [von Neumann] proposal to build a computing machine here at the Institute. I respect his belief that such a device will open up whole new vistas of understanding of phenomena like the weather, fluid flow, and perhaps even economic processes. Johnny's scientific judgment is seldom wrong and I would never bet against it. But the Institute is not the right place for such a project. I have been here since the earliest days, and I know that the founders, especially Mr. Flexner, would not have entertained for a moment the idea of an *engineering* project being done here."

Oppenheimer listened impassively to this plea, nodding his head from time to time as Weyl made the argument for the Platonic nature of the IAS as a home for the most rarefied of abstract, speculative thought, and outlined his reasons for opposing von Neumann's proposal, which had been made to the faculty of mathematics just a few weeks earlier.

After a moment's pause, Oppenheimer said softly, "Hermann, I fully understand the principle underlying your argument. Everyone here has the highest regard and greatest respect for Johnny's belief that building a computing machine is something worth doing. But many of the mathematicians like yourself, Marston [Morse], and Deane [Montgomery] think that such a project is out of place and out of the spirit of what this Institute is all about. Others, such as Einstein, don't think such a device will help their work in any way and remain indifferent to the whole notion."

"But you are the Director, Robert. How do *you* feel about it?" pleaded Weyl. "Your position is certain to have a great influence on how the trustees think about this proposal. And make no mistake, I'm sure this adventure of Johnny's will ultimately have to be decided by the trustees. Faculty emotions are running so high that I don't see how you can decide it one way or the other without alienating many of them."

Oppenheimer had to agree. "I am really torn between two diametrically opposed principles. On the one hand, the Institute was founded on a deeply held belief in the value of purely theoretical research. In Mr. Flexner's manifesto selling the idea of the Institute to the Bamberger family, he explicitly stated that applied work of any sort would not be welcome here."

"Precisely," said Weyl, moving in for the kill. "Applied work can be done in many places, and the small staff and resources of the IAS certainly cannot compete with large government labs or even university or industrial research departments in doing applied experiments and developing commercial products."

"Yes," agreed Oppie, "but there is another side to this coin, the principle that an IAS professor like Johnny should be free to pursue his research Muse wherever she may lead him. If the IAS stands for anything, it stands for total and complete freedom of choice on what problems to think about and on what methods to employ for their solution—even to the construction of a computing machine. I'm sure you understand."

"Of course I understand. But we all assume that someone appointed to a professorship here at least tacitly accepts the principles under which the Institute was chartered and operates. One of the most sacrosanct is that applied work is simply not done here. Johnny is now calling this principle into question with this computing project."

Oppenheimer thought back to his discussions with von Neumann about the computing machine and questioned whether Johnny would have agreed with the label "applied" or "engineering" for this activity. While the machine he wanted to build could certainly be thought of as a tool for doing calculations, hence applied work, the actual design and construction would be very far from a routine, well-worked-out engineering exercise. Only a handful of computing machines had ever been constructed, each one very different in design and physical structure from the others.

The crux of the matter lay in the fact that such a machine would be a tool foreign to the ways the mathematicians and theoretical physicists traditionally plied their trade. Oppenheimer saw clearly that what bothered these folks, great as their intellect and accomplishments were, was the threat the computing machine posed to their way of practicing their profession.

Rather than confront Weyl with this directly, he said, "This is a very difficult and delicate issue, Hermann, and I am going to have to give the entire matter considerably more thought. I'm sure you would be the first to agree that Johnny is one of our preeminent faculty members and I do not want to get into a position of telling him how to carry on his research. But I am very sensitive, as well, to the concerns you and others have expressed about this project being done here at the IAS. We will just have to think a bit longer and a bit harder to see if we can come to an accommodation that everyone can live with."

Glancing at the clock on the wall over the doorway of the Commons Room, Oppenheimer quickly closed the discussion, telling Weyl, "I'm afraid you'll have to excuse me now. I have a visitor from the Atomic Energy Commission due in my office in just two minutes. I appreciate your expressing your views on von Neumann's project to me directly. We will take up the matter again very soon."

Chapter Three

GOODTIME JOHNNY

The elegant white lodge house at 26 Wescott Road was known far and wide among the Princeton cognescenti as the place for the best parties in town. A passerby, hearing the music and conversation pouring out of the windows open to the street, would be surprised to learn that the host was not some New York banker or Philadelphia industrialist, but of all things, a mathematician! But the house's resident was no ordinary mathematician. Not by a long shot. John Louis von Neumann was a mathematician's mathematician, a child genius who, instead of burning out as an adult as do many mathematicians, set a blazing fire in every corner of the intellectual forest his fertile mind touched.

Nevertheless, what "Johnny" liked best (after thinking, that is) was partying! This warm, spring night was typical of his social life, as the short, pudgy von Neumann and his equally short, dark-haired, vivacious wife, Klari, welcomed their guests at the front door. Von Neumann ushered them into the large, black-and-white checkerboard-tiled foyer, with his customary courtly, central European manners. With a welcoming smile, von Neumann took pains to ensure that everyone was properly pointed in the direction of the bar set up in the kitchen. Dressed in his characteristic three-piece gray pinstripe suit and silk, patterned necktie, he looked more like a man ready to give solemn testimony before a congressional budget committee than the convivial host of an informal cocktail party at his own home. But that formal exterior hid a natural-born partyer, as everyone in Princeton knew well by now.

Von Neumann was especially pleased that his closest friend and fellow central European emigré, Stanislaw Ulam, was visiting the Institute from Los Alamos that week. Ulam would be arriving shortly, and there was much for them to catch up on. He was particularly eager to hear the news from New Mexico about how people at "the Labs" (the Los Alamos Laboratories) were thinking about the development of atomic weapons. Even though the war was over, von Neumann was deeply concerned with the growing threat posed by the totalitarian left wing in Russia. And in contrast to Oppenheimer, Einstein, and most of the other academics in Princeton, he strongly endorsed the accelerated development of the hydrogen fusion bomb, nicknamed the "Super," as one way to put a damper on Soviet expansionist tendencies.

Drawn from the bar in the kitchen by the soft, almost liquid, sounds of Benny Goodman's magical clarinet coming from the phonograph in the corner of the living room, the portly, balding Viennese economist Oskar Morgenstern rejoined the party, a puzzled frown on his sombre face. Yet one more intellectual from *Mitteleuropa* who had taken refuge from war-torn Europe at the IAS, Morgenstern thought back to a conversation he had had with von Neumann earlier that day. The two were putting the finishing touches on one of the chapters in their magisterial work on rational behavior and economics, when von Neumann made the offhand remark that to produce decisive results in the field of economics, mathematical tools comparable in magnitude and importance to the calculus would have to be discovered. Of a slightly Napoleanic turn of mind anyway, Morgenstern interpreted this to mean that the theory of games of strategy he and von Neumann were developing at that very moment might well serve as this new kind of mathematics. He hoped that perhaps he'd have a chance to pick the great man's brain a bit more on this topic during the evening.

As von Neumann bustled in from the hallway to join the party, which was already in full swing, one of the guests smiled and handed him a small gift-wrapped box. "I think you'll enjoy this," said the guest, a physicist whom von Neumann had met at the Institute but whose name—like almost everyone's name—the great man's prodigious memory simply could not recall. Warmly thanking the man for the present, von Neumann's face beamed when he unwrapped it and saw inside one of those thermodynamic birds that sits on the edge of a glass of water and dips its beak into the water in a metronomic fashion, depending on whether its beak is wet from the water or dried out from evaporation. Von Neumann immediately got a glassful of water and set the bird on the fireplace mantel, declaring a new house rule: "Whenever the bird drinks," he cried, "we all have to drink, too." He quickly grabbed a glass and poured himself a full measure of Scotch whisky to get this new tradition off to a proper start.

"Tell us, Johnny," said one of the other guests, turning the conversation serious for a moment, "as someone who grew up next door to the Russians, what do you think about their intentions in central Europe now that the war is over?"

Von Neumann's soft, almost cherubic face changed suddenly from that of a jovial party host to that of a very sober, sombre man. Pondering in silence for a moment, he stated quite directly and unequivocally, "The Russians are now entrenched throughout central Europe. History shows that once they occupy a country, they never peacefully leave it. Sooner or later there will be a great conflict between them and us."

"Do you believe we should use our superiority in atomic weapons right now to push them out of central Europe?" pressed the questioner, as several other partygoers gathered around to eavesdrop on this interchange.

"I am certainly no advocate of preemptive strikes against any country—usually," von Neumann began. "But the Western way of life, whose preservation was what this great war was all about, is threatened by Soviet hegemony in central Europe," he went on with the utmost gravity. "I'm sure no one here needs reminding of what Churchill said in Missouri just a few weeks ago. 'An iron curtain has descended across the continent.' Europe has now been divided into East and West. The West is going to have to defend the freedoms won by the war against this encroachment by Stalin. So in this case I say the sooner we strike, the smaller the eventual price in human suffering and death."

"In other words, strike now while we have the clear advantage?" continued the questioner, relentlessly pressing von Neumann.

"Absolutely," said von Neumann, clearly uncomfortable with the turn this conversation was taking. Looking for a way to escape the sobering discussion, he glanced up at the mantelpiece and said cheerfully, "I see our little bird has just dipped its beak into the glass, so perhaps we should all return to the bar and do the same."

(On Christmas Day of that year, just a few months after von Neumann's prophetic statement about Soviet intentions, the Russians achieved their first nuclear chain reaction. This was the outcome of a crash effort by Soviet scientists to gain parity with the United States following the spectacular atomic weapons tests at Bikini Atoll earlier in the summer. There can be no doubt it was these two events that catalyzed the United Nations to create an international atomic energy agency to promote and oversee the peaceful uses of nuclear energy over Soviet objections calling for nuclear disarmament before any such agency could be created. Von Neumann's concern over Russian expansionism led him to play a central role in the American nuclear program until the end of his life.)

⋮

Suddenly, almost out of nowhere it seemed, a short, slightly balding, dark-haired man in a rumpled gray sports jacket appeared at von Neumann's side, an enigmatic smile on his face. Glancing over at him, von Neumann's face lit up in welcome as he reached out to embrace the new arrival in a display of affection that was rare for the normally reserved, rather formal von Neumann.

"Stan!" he cried. "It's wonderful to have you back in Princeton again. I've been looking forward to your coming back to us. I hope you will be able to stay a bit longer this time, so we can talk a bit."

Stan Ulam knew Princeton well from his stay at the Institute in the mid-1930s, shortly after its formation, and long before he took up a position in Los Alamos as part of the Manhattan Project. He was now "genius-in-residence" at Los Alamos, the type of mathematician who is completely at home in a variety of areas in both pure and applied math—topology, mathematical logic, differential equations, probability theory, statistics—and with a deep interest as well in the applications of computing machines to the exploration of mathematical structures in physics and biology. It was during their time together in Princeton and then Los Alamos that he and von Neumann had become the best of friends, and their families still spent summer holidays together in New Mexico and other parts of western America.

"I just got into town today, Johnny," he replied, "and got your invitation at the hotel. Even after a transcontinental trip, I'm never too tired for a night at the von Neumanns. So I rushed right over. We all know that a party at Johnny and Klari's is the best show in town." Looking around at the guests filling up the house, Ulam continued, "I can already see I'm not to be disappointed."

"Indeed, you will not be disappointed. Come to the kitchen with me and I'll get you fixed up with a drink. Besides, there's something I need to ask you about," said von Neumann as he grabbed him by the elbow and steered him toward the bar.

Von Neumann stood at the kitchen counter mixing a potent-looking Scotch-and-soda. As he turned and handed it to Ulam, they clinked glasses and von Neumann spoke in a low tone that allowed no doubt as to the gravity of what he was about to say.

"Stan, you know I've been increasingly frustrated by the attitude of the Institute faculty toward my proposal to build a computing machine here. It simply mystifies me how such otherwise intelligent people can be so blind when it comes to the implications of this technology for changing our way of doing science."

Ulam raised his eyebrows over the rim of his glass and nodded.

"Tell me, Johnny, who is objecting and do they have any real basis for their opposition, other than that a computing machine is a *machine* and it represents a threat to their usual way of doing business here in this one, true, Platonic heaven?"

"Well, Morse says that he sees the computer as inevitable —but far from optimum. Einstein jokes that he doesn't see how a computer will bring him any closer to a unified field theory. Then Siegel makes the inane objection that when he needs a logarithm he prefers to compute it by hand rather than look it up in a table. A table! As if the computer were nothing but a glorified calculating machine!"

"Strange, actually," Ulam agreed with a smile, "since *I* think the computer is very much like a telescope, not a calculating machine at all. A telescope enables us to see things the naked eye cannot. The computer will enable us to see things that are invisible—or rather, inaccessible—to the unaided brain. Nevertheless, the faculty sounds as if they're completely indifferent to your arguments, Johnny."

"*Indifference* is putting far too kind a face on it," von Neumann replied in a huff. "They are not only indifferent, they're blind to how technology changes everything. But I still have a card or two to play in this game, Stan, and I will certainly play them as skillfully as I can—at just the right moment."

Ulam smiled to himself at this remark. Vintage Johnny, he thought. Always ready to tackle the most difficult problem. And never afraid to stand up for his ideas, which are almost always years—no, decades—ahead of their time. Sometimes he wondered if von Neumann was human at all. Perhaps he was really an alien from a "second Earth" on the other side of the galaxy, who had made a detailed study of humans and could imitate them perfectly. His mind seemed so far ahead of everyone else's. Even the other geniuses at the Institute were going to be left in the dust by Johnny's computer project.

"Enough of our problems. Either they'll be solved or I'll take the project somewhere else. Tell me the news from Los Alamos, Stan. What are you working on now out there in your desert hideaway?"

Ulam looked thoughtfully and a bit soberly out the window, gazing at the carefree partyers, laughing and drinking in the back garden, before replying.

"You know, Johnny, [Edward] Teller is intent on building the 'Super' [the hydrogen bomb]. And there are a lot of others who support his reasoning that we have to do it to keep the Russians in check. I'm sure you number yourself among that group. And a computer like the one you're proposing is absolutely essential to carry out the calculations we need to show us how to build it."

Here Ulam was referring to the fact that building a workable hydrogen bomb requires understanding the flow of gas plasmas at densities and temperatures rivaling those in the interior of the sun. While it is possible to write down the mathematical equations describing these quantities, it is not possible to solve them in terms of elementary functions such as polynomials, exponentials, or trigonometric functions. So the only way to obtain the solutions is to numerically compute them directly from the equations. But the volume of calculations needed to do this is beyond the capability of even an army of human "computers" hard at work with mechanical desk calculators. Only the type of electronic computer von Neumann was proposing could do them.

Von Neumann nodded enthusiastically, saying, "I always knew that, Stan. This is precisely the type of problem I had in mind when I took up the work with Mauchly and Eckert in Philadelphia on the ENIAC during the war. The computer opens up a whole new world to us, one in which we will be able to literally *see* the solutions to real-life problems in physics. This is one of those problems. That's why I find it so mystifying that the faculty here at the IAS is so indifferent to the whole idea."

"Yes," agreed Ulam, trying to shift the focus of the conversation a bit. "The ladies who 'computed' for the Manhattan

Project could not in several lifetimes have ever completed the computations needed for building the Super."

Both men mused silently for a moment on those hectic—but now almost halcyon—days on the mesa in Los Alamos, when the "computers" consisted of a roomful of wives of the scientists, hunched over mechanical calculators, each churning out a piece of an overall calculation whose grand structure had been planned by von Neumann. As one not at all averse to the sight of a well-turned ankle or the curve of a rounded bosom, von Neumann occasionally thought back to that time with great pleasure. And now here with his best friend, Ulam, those memories came back in a rush—but only momentarily. Then he was off again to ride his latest hobbyhorse, selling the virtues of an electronic computer even to the already-converted.

"Stan, you know as well as anyone that the question of how fluids move to create a nuclear explosion is not much different from the question of how fluids move in the atmosphere to create weather. I want to use the computer we build here in Princeton to understand and control the weather, not to design weapons."

Ulam thought this was a pretty tall order, controlling the weather, but kept the thought to himself. Again, though, he smiled inwardly at how completely typical this was of Johnny's boundless faith in his mind's ability to understand anything, even the weather, if it behaved according to a set of rules. If there was a rational pattern underlying any natural or human behavior, Johnny believed it must be comprehensible and explainable by the methods of science.

"But we'll have time for more discussion of these matters in the next few days before you return to New Mexico. So let's get back to the party before the food disappears completely," he said, directing Ulam to the living room with a broad sweep of his arm.

In his mention of the ENIAC work (carried out just after the war at the Moore School at the University of Pennsylvania in Philadelphia), von Neumann was referring to the first large-scale electronic computer ever built in America. Von Neumann's report on the logical structure and operation of that machine served as the blueprint for several similar computing machines built for the military and for nuclear research facilities. Believing strongly in openness and the sharing of scientific knowledge, his idea of building an improved version of the ENIAC at the IAS was to provide such a machine for purely scientific purposes.

The type of machine he envisioned for the IAS would be a "parallel" machine, operating on quantities stored in the binary digits ("bits") 0 and 1, not the decimal digits 0 through 9. The parallel architecture meant that the machine would carry out several computations at once, rather than just a single operation during each of its clock cycles. It would have approximately 2,300 vacuum tubes for its active circuitry, with an electrostatic memory of 1,024 words, each 440 bits long. Von Neumann also planned to make use of a magnetic drum to serve as "slow," bulk memory for the machine. He thought the computer would take about three years to build, assuming a staff of ten people to do the logical design, development of hardware, and other associated tasks.

$$\vdots$$

By the time von Neumann and Ulam got back to the food it had almost all been vacuumed up by the voracious guests. But they managed to salvage a few crumbs of cheese and a tired-looking bit of bread and salmon. As they made do with these leftovers, a sandy-haired, young physicist of medium height approached von Neumann timidly and said, "Professor von Neumann, let me introduce myself. My name is David Bohm.

I'm visiting the Physics Department here at the university and am a colleague of Professor Wigner, who suggested that I ask you about something that's troubling me in my work on quantum theory."

Von Neumann, who was unfailingly polite to Nobel laureates and graduate students alike, looked up at the shy, self-effacing Bohm and bowed like an Old World courtier as he shook Bohm's hand and smiled in an attempt to put him at ease. "Did you know that Wigner and I attended the same grammar school in Budapest?"

"Yes, Professor Wigner mentioned that. He said you were already a legend at the school even in his class, which I believe was a year or two behind your own."

Shaking his head at the mention of being a "legend," von Neumann smiled and asked Bohm how he could help him with his work.

"Well," said Bohm, struggling to get his thoughts in order. "I have been troubled by the question of the meaning conventional quantum theory attaches to the question of the status of a particle like an electron when it is not actually being observed."

"Yes?" encouraged von Neumann with a nod.

"The difficulty for me is that the commonly accepted view seems to be that attributes of the electron like position and momentum simply do not exist until they are brought into existence through an act of observation."

"It is difficult to escape that interpretation when you try to match the mathematics of quantum theory with the actual experimental results," agreed von Neumann.

"But how can that be?" queried Bohm. "How can a definite physical object like an electron literally have no properties, even something as basic as a location in space and time, until it is observed? It makes no sense. And what is to count as an observer? A human being? A photographic plate? A lowly cockroach? I know that you have thought longer and harder about this question than almost anyone and I'd like to know what you think about this perplexing question."

Von Neumann had indeed pondered this conundrum— for a very long time. He had been especially troubled by when, *exactly,* a property like an electron's position comes into existence from the smeared-out fog of possible positions and their corresponding probabilities described by the electron's so-called wave function. This purely mathematical object, obeying the famed Schrödinger equation, can be interpreted as a wave of probability characterizing where the electron would be found when an observation, or measurement, was actually performed. But at what moment in the process of carrying out the measurement does the probability become a certainty? *That* is the question von Neumann had thought deeply about for more than 20 years. Looking intently at Bohm, he gave the younger man the distilled essence of those deliberations.

"The real question, my friend, is where you put the 'cut' between the system being measured, an electron, for instance, and the system doing the measuring. The exact value of the electron's position comes into existence at *some* stage of the measurement process. I think we all concur on that."

"Yes," agreed Bohm. "But if you regard both the electron and the measuring system as quantum objects, then the wave function, which has a spectrum of values before any observation of the electron, degenerates, or we might say 'collapses,' to a single value somewhere between the two, doesn't it?"

"Precisely. But when you work out the mathematics, it turns out not to matter where you put the cut. As far as the final observed result goes, the wave function collapse can occur in the electron, in the measuring system, or anywhere in between."

This startling result, the so-called "Cut Theorem," led von Neumann to focus on the one slightly fishy element in the whole measurement chain: the human mind. He told Bohm, "In my opinion, since you can regard the process of the wave probability characterized by the wave function collapsing into a single value as taking place anywhere, the real 'collapsor' of the wave function can only be human consciousness. Only when the measurement enters into the consciousness of a human observer does the electron really acquire a well-defined position."

By now several other guests had wandered in from the backyard and from other corners of the house to gather around and listen to von Neumann and Bohm discuss this exotic question coming from the twilight zone where modern physics meets philosophy. Just as von Neumann was explaining the final point of his consciousness-based theory of quantum reality, a commotion broke out on the other side of the living room. Priding himself on harmony above all else at his parties and hearing the raised voices and general disturbance, von Neumann abandoned Bohm and walked over to the other group to see what the ruckus was all about. Bohm followed, rather like a loyal dog following his master's lead.

The group clustered near the fireplace was composed of the mathematician Hermann Weyl, the economist Oskar Morgenstern, the young British physicist Freeman Dyson, and Ulam. As von Neumann joined them, Dyson was in the midst of excitedly arguing a point of epistemology to Morgenstern in a firm voice strongly betraying his British origins.

"I accept your claim, Morgenstern, that there is a greater certainty of knowledge in mathematics than in physics. After all, physics is about the real world of matter and energy, not about abstract relationships and logical consistency. But I most certainly do not accept the idea that there is no more real knowledge in physics than in a field like economics. The closer one comes to areas where human decisions and foibles enter in a central way, the farther one is from the kind of knowledge one might term 'scientific.' "

Despite a childhood in the same final days of the courtly Habsburg central European empire that shaped von Neumann's youth, Morgenstern's demeanor was by no means courtly or diplomatic—especially when he was arguing a point of philosophy or science. He went straight for the jugular, making no exceptions even for a young scientist like Dyson, still wet behind his philosophical ears.

"All right, then, Mr. Dyson, just tell me, please, what exactly you have in mind when you speak about 'scientific knowledge.' Is that some refined, exalted type of knowledge going beyond the brand of knowledge we obtain from art, music, literature, or any of the other means humans employ to create our realities?"

Hearing this interchange, von Neumann's ears perked up. It was exactly the same question—but framed in a more general way—as the one he had just been discussing with Bohm: Is there such a thing as "scientific knowledge"? And if so, how does that type of knowledge differ from the knowledge of the world expressed by the poet, economist, writer, or musician? He could not hold back from the discussion.

"Gentlemen, gentlemen, let us elevate the tone of this debate and consider this fascinating topic using our intellects, and not try to win debating points simply by the volume of our voices. My young friend here, Mr. Bohm, and I have just been considering a special form of your general question about scientific knowledge in the context of quantum theory and what that theory tells us about what can actually be known about the attributes of an electron. Perhaps we can fit this question into the broader issue you are discussing here."

At Weyl's urging, von Neumann then explained the problem with measurement that he and Bohm had been considering, whereupon Ulam raised the obvious issue of what is meant by "knowledge" of any kind. The fat was really in the fire now, as everyone in the group vied to be the first to put forward his own idiosyncratic answer to this seemingly simple query.

"I take a very pragmatic view of this matter," said Ulam forcefully, his faint Polish accent becoming more evident the more excited he became. "For me, knowledge is what you get when you receive the answer to a question."

Dyson interjected instantly: "But anyone can give an answer. It certainly can't really be knowledge if the answer is incomplete, ambiguous, or just plain wrong. There has to be some kind of general agreement that the answer is a good and complete one for you to say you've gained knowledge from it. But how does that consensus arise?"

Weyl stepped in to quietly answer Dyson's question. Calling for the group's attention by gently tapping the side of his glass, he declared, "Your problem about who validates an answer is something Ludwig Wittgenstein agonized over for decades. Finally, Wittgenstein concluded that the acceptability of an answer ultimately came from the collective opinion of a social group. So if the question were, say, von Neumann's puzzle about quantum measurement, then the only acceptable answer would come from the community of quantum physicists and philosophers of science agreeing on a resolution of the dilemma. But, of course, they don't."

Von Neumann then moved the discussion forward by proposing that, for the sake of argument, they agree that knowledge comes from a valid answer to a question. "What then," he said, "is the difference between general knowledge and knowledge we gain using the tools of science?"

Speaking ever more rapidly, Ulam argued that there is indeed a difference. "First of all, scientific answers come from following a set of rules," he claimed. "But not just any set of rules will do. For instance, the Ten Commandments is a set of rules. And these rules even provide the answers to questions, such as, Can I steal this car? But no one would consider these answers to be in any way 'scientific.' "

"What, then, separates the scientific answer to the question about an electron's position coming from following a rule such as that specified by the Schrödinger equation, and the answer about stealing a car coming from the Ten Commandments?" asked Dyson.

"I think the difference rests in two different aspects of these rules that set them apart from rules in general. The first is the special properties of the rules themselves, while the second is in the way in which the rule is arrived at," replied Ulam.

Everyone looked at Ulam expecting him to explain what he meant by scientific rules having special properties. First peering into his empty whisky glass as if seeking revelation at the bottom, Ulam finally looked up at Dyson and continued in a rather serious, low voice, "Scientific rules do have properties distinguishing them from something like the Ten Commandments. For instance, they are *explicit*. There is little ambiguity in what something like the Schrödinger equation means. Anyone with even a bit of training in mathematics and physics has no trouble at all in agreeing on what the rule means."

"Yes," nodded Morgenstern, who had been uncharacteristically silent during this discussion. "But what about *objectivity?* Can you say that is a property of a scientific rule?"

"Well, perhaps. But I think that term could be interpreted in two very different ways," replied Ulam. "One would be that the rule exists independently of any human investigator, something like how some mathematicians think of the number π having a bona fide existence in some Platonic realm beyond space and time. But there is also the weaker notion that a rule is objective if it is simply independent of investigator bias or prejudice."

"What do you mean by this second interpretation?" asked

Weyl.

"Simply that the rule is what it is and is not something that depends on, say, the politics of the investigator or the status of his bank account or his position in the scientific hierarchy. So, for instance, the exponent in Newton's inverse-square law of gravitation is 2 and not any other number, regardless of who the investigator studying gravitational theory is or of his or her social status. That's what I mean by 'objectivity.' And scientific rules have it; those in other areas may or may not."

At this point, the group started adding other properties characteristic of scientific rules: *reliability, public availability, compactness,* and so on. Finally, von Neumann asked Ulam about his second filter for separating scientific rules from the pretenders.

"Stan, you said that scientific rules not only had special properties but that they were also created in a special way. What did you have in mind?"

"That's easy. All of us here know very well that the entire edifice of science rests upon what we call *the scientific method:* the way we go from empirical observations to a hypothesis and then testing the hypothesis in controlled, repeatable experiments to accept or reject it. The hypotheses that survive this process then get put together into what I would call a 'scientific' rule."

So there it was. The criteria by which scientific rules are generated. And, thus, the way scientific knowledge parts company from knowledge in general. Simply answering questions by invoking scientific rules. But von Neumann was not quite satisfied. He asked Ulam, "That's all well and good, Stan. I don't think any of us here really disagrees with you. But if the scientific answer to a question comes from applying a scientific rule, then this sounds very much like doing science is the same thing as doing a calculation. Just feed the question into the machine, the scientific rule, turn the handle of the machine, and the scientific answer pops out the other end. Is that it? Is that all there is to science?"

In a rather skeptical tone, someone then added from the back of the group, "If the practice of science is finding a scientific rule to answer a question, then isn't science in the same boat as mathematics? After all, Gödel showed that there is more to mathematics than simply following rules. There are mathematical truths that just cannot be accessed by applying a fixed set of rules."

"Precisely," added Weyl, with a gleam in his eye. "That would also imply then that there are truths about the real world that cannot be found or seen using the methodology of science, since that methodology is also rule-based."

Here was the nub of the matter. Both Ulam and von Neumann were arguing vigorously for science being a way to create a reality by discovering, then applying, a set of rules. Von Neumann, of course, had his computer in mind as the quintessential rule-following device. It took him about three milliseconds to point this out to the assembled audience.

"It is almost certainly true that there are sound logical reasons to believe that there are questions about humans and nature that are beyond the bounds of science. But turn the matter around. *If* science really is essentially the carrying out of a calculation, then the limits of science are necessarily extended whenever we extend our computational capabilities. The computer promises to do this in a way that has never been seen before. That's as good an argument as I can offer for having such a computing machine here at the IAS, don't you think?"

Stony silence greeted this obvious sales pitch by von Neumann for his computing project. It seemed no one really wanted to either endorse the idea or speak against it, since the group consisted of supporters of both sides. Besides, who could speak out against a host as genial and welcoming as

Johnny? Finally, Morgenstern broke the silence saying, "Following Gödel's work, we've found a lot of problems in mathematics that defy resolution by following a set of logical rules. But can anyone here suggest a question from physics or from the social realm that seems to be a problem whose solution is beyond the bounds of science?"

The guests digested this question in silence for a few moments. Finally, Dyson said cheerfully, "Here's a possibility. What about the Three-Body Problem from celestial mechanics?" He was referring to the problem posed by three celestial bodies like the Sun, Earth, and Moon moving with respect to each other's gravitational fields. Given the initial positions and velocities of the three bodies, the question is whether, after some finite amount of time, a collision between two of the bodies will occur, or if one of the bodies will exceed some predefined velocity, perhaps great enough for the object to escape the pull of the other two and fly off into interstellar space. The problem had been solved long ago for the case of two bodies (mathematically, at least). But it remained open for any system of three or more bodies.

Weyl immediately remarked, "Of course, you have to draw a distinction here between a solution to this problem in a mathematical sense, involving idealized point particles moving in a frictionless environment, and real planetary bodies moving in the physical universe."

"Naturally," agreed Dyson. "But we don't even have a solution for the idealized mathematical case."

"Besides, how would you ever verify in the physical case whether there was a set of rules that could answer the question?" added Morgenstern. "I might propose any number of such puzzles from economics, too, for example, the efficiency of a financial market. How could you ever say whether a real financial market like the New York Stock Exchange is efficient?"

By "efficiency," Morgenstern was referring to the way prices move in response to new information that comes to the attention of investors. A perfectly efficient market would instantaneously process such information and assimilate it into the price of a security.

"This is the type of issue that separates mathematicians from physicists and philosophers," asserted Weyl forcefully. "In mathematics we have the notion of *proof*, which enables us to state unequivocally that certain propositions cannot be proved or disproved. But what is the analogue of proof in the physical world? To claim that something is beyond the bounds of science, you need to put something in place that serves the same role that proof does in mathematics."

Ulam fidgeted nervously for a moment, finally remarking, "Well, my idea was not to cross the boundary from mathematics to physics—or economics—but just to stay within the framework of computation. So I'm really only concerned with 'science' insofar as we deal with a mathematical model of reality, not reality itself. Life in the real world is much too difficult."

Just as this remark seemed to set the cat among the pigeons, promising a lively debate, a flurry of activity at the archway between the living room and the rest of the house attracted the group's attention. Klari von Neumann and a gaggle of other wives bustled into the room, looking daggers at the men.

"You men have been neglecting the ladies long enough," she said, leaving no room for debate on the matter. "You can all think your great thoughts tomorrow. This is a party, not the Institute tearoom. It's time to dance, drink, and relax."

Even the great von Neumann had to acknowledge the existence of this greater force, as he bowed to his wife's dictum and told the group, "This is definitely a theme we must return to soon. But Klari is right. We are here for a party, not an

Institute seminar. So let us join the ladies and continue our discussion another day."

As the group disbanded and made their way to the kitchen, back patio, and other corners of the house, von Neumann buttonholed Weyl and asked for a brief word. He spoke softly in German, not wanting this conversation to attract attention from the others.

"You know, Hermann, Gödel's case for promotion to Professor is on the agenda for our next faculty meeting. I know you have doubts about the lasting value of his work. Nevertheless, I do not believe that even you can say that his work is not of the highest caliber. And I ask for your support when we discuss this promotion."

"My reservations about Gödel's work have nothing whatsoever to do with its quality. They rest purely on the philsophical basis of the work, not the work itself," replied Weyl. "Gödel is certainly the greatest logician of our time."

"Yes," said von Neumann. "I sometimes wonder how any of us can call ourselves 'Professor' if Gödel can not."

Weyl cautioned von Neumann quietly. "Johnny, you, of all people, should know that being a Professor at the Institute is much more than just doing outstanding intellectual work. The position entails many organizational and administrative chores, arranging seminars, selecting visitors for the coming year, and so forth. Do you really want someone with Gödel's legalistic turn of mind to be involved in these mundane—but essential—chores?"

"I'm just saying that it's embarrassing for the Institute to have Gödel on our faculty in any position lower than that of Professor. And, yes, I am ready to accept whatever additional administrative burden having him involved in these day-to-day activities may impose on the rest of us."

"I'm not sure I am," demurred Weyl. "But I will think about it between now and the faculty meeting."

"Thank you. Now I think I see Klari casting an evil look our way from the doorway. Perhaps we'd better rejoin the party."

Chapter Four

GÖDEL AT THE BLACKBOARD

J ohn von Neumann had the fastest, most logical mind of the twentieth century. So when he analyzed a problem there was never any doubt in anybody's mind as to what needed to be done. This morning as he drove his shiny, new, blue Cadillac to work, that razor-sharp mind was focused on the vexing problem of Gödel's promotion. What could he do to overcome the resistance of his colleagues in the School of Mathematics to what he saw as an open-and-shut case? Indeed, how could any of them call themselves "Professor" if Gödel could not? Passing "Von Neumann's corner," an intersection famed in Princeton for the number of times the great man had wrapped his car around a particularly stubborn tree there when his flights of mental fancy distracted his thoughts from the steering wheel, von Neumann suddenly had an inspiration. He would organize a presentation. Not just your everyday, plain vanilla type of IAS seminar. No, nothing so dry and formal and academic. Rather, he would persuade Gödel to present a popular account of his greatest work to the faculty and Institute visitors. And he would arrange for this public relations effort to occur just before the faculty meeting at which Gödel's case for promotion was to be considered. Von Neumann thought that by hearing directly from Gödel himself about his stunning achievements in logic, the faculty would be softened up for the pitch he would then make at the meeting in support of Gödel's promotion.

Fired with enthusiasm, von Neumann drove through the infamous intersection, smiling just a bit when he recalled his last fiasco at this corner. When asked by the police how he had managed to run straight into a tree on a sunny, dry, autumn morning, von Neumann replied that the trees were proceeding in an orderly fashion at 60 miles per hour past his window—when one of them suddenly jumped out in front of him! No wonder he bought a new Cadillac every year. Arriving at the Institute parking area, he jumped from the car and bustled across the lot into Fuld Hall to set about implementing his plan for Gödel's "sales presentation."

The first hurdle I'll have to jump, thought von Neumann, is to persuade Gödel himself to suggest giving the talk. He knew that a direct approach would be futile, because the ever more reclusive Gödel would undoubtedly cringe at the idea of making any type of public presentation, especially one that he saw as overtly self-promotional. So something far subtler would be needed to convince Gödel that his interests would be served by such a talk. Von Neumann's lightning-quick analysis immediately presented the answer: Discreetly hint to Gödel that some of the faculty members objecting to his promotion didn't really believe his work shed much light on the foundations of mathematics, but rather was more of a semantic parlor trick in logic. Von Neumann was certain that would infuriate Gödel, who would then insist on presenting his work to the faculty. He would want to set it in context and outline the importance of the work for understanding the limitations of the human brain's ability to access mathematical "deep reality."

As fate would have it, von Neumann's assistant happened to mention as they exchanged morning greetings how odd it was to see Gödel coming into the Institute that morning completely wrapped up in a heavy scarf and overcoat when the sun was shining and the mercury was already rising to an uncomfortable level for a late-spring day in Princeton. Knowing now that Gödel was in the Institute, von Neumann immediately set off down the corridor to Gödel's office to put his plan into action.

.
.

Among Gödel's many eccentricities, the bleak sparseness of his office ranked high. Entering the room at Gödel's not entirely friendly response, "Who's there?" to the knock on his closed door, von Neumann saw Gödel lying on a kind of divan in the corner. The window shades were drawn, so that the room was in semi-darkness on this bright, sunny morning. Besides the divan, the only other furniture in the room was a desk with a rather worn leather desk chair, a completely bare wooden bookcase behind the desk, a blackboard wiped clean, and a simple wooden chair. All in all, a perfect imitation of a police interrogation room. All that was missing was an ashtray overflowing with half-smoked cigarettes and a few bloodstains on the wall. Well, thought von Neumann, who needs books, a table, and chairs for small meetings, small talk, or anything else when all you do is *think?* This was not going to be easy, he realized, as he began his oblique pitch to the Grand Exalted Ruler of the Platonic Realm.

"I'm very pleased to see you here today, Kurt. This morning I had an idea about the philosophical basis of mathematical logic, and I wanted to get your opinion about it."

"You know, Johnny, that I'm not as active in this field as I once was. But I will try to help. What's on your mind?"

"Well," von Neumann began, taking a seat in the chair in front of the desk and wondering if Gödel deliberately chose such an uncomfortable chair to discourage the few visitors he had from lingering. "I was speaking about your incompleteness results with one of our esteemed colleagues recently, who said that while he greatly admired the virtuosity of your work, he felt that what your results demonstrate is not so much the limitations of mathematical reasoning, but that your belief in the actual *existence* of the answer to an undecideable proposition is simply not the right way to think about the 'reality' of a mathematical object."

Gödel's face darkened, as he let loose one of his strange high-pitched laughs, something between a witch's cackle and a giggle. Waving his hand in a dismissive gesture he said, "I suppose you were talking with some constructivist. These people have been arguing for a long time that the type of undecideable propositions that my work implies must exist have no mathematical reality at all, since they cannot be *constructed* in a finite way. In other words, they cannot be built up directly from the positive integers by a finite number of operations like addition, subtraction, and so forth."

"Precisely my point, Kurt," said von Neumann immediately, sensing an opening to put forward his idea that Gödel give a lecture straightening out the skeptics on these matters. "I think these constructivists have too narrow a view of mathematical truth. Someone needs to present a clear picture of where they have gone astray. Maybe an Institute seminar on mathematical truth would be a good way to do it. That would at least clear the air on these foundational matters here in Princeton. Yes, this type of public airing of the dispute would be a very good thing. How do you feel about that, Kurt?"

Gödel's face took on a thousand-yard stare, as he opened one of the shades and gazed off into the trees beyond the lawn outside his office window, pondering von Neumann's idea. Eager to push Gödel to volunteer to deliver such a talk, von Neumann added: "You know, this lecture would be very helpful in moving forward your candidacy for a professorship here, since it would help overcome some of the obstacles raised in the faculty meetings about how important your work really is."

This remark instantly got Gödel's attention, and he turned to von Neumann and said sharply, "I don't want someone else explaining my work, Johnny. If anyone is going to do that it's going to be me."

Smiling inwardly at how easily he had maneuvered Gödel into this declaration, von Neumann announced, "Excellent. I could not agree more. You are the only one to do it. I will set up the talk as the next colloquium lecture in the School of Mathematics. My assistant will tell you the date later today."

Von Neumann glanced quickly at his wristwatch, eager to escape from Gödel before there could be any debate or, even worse, a change of heart. "I have a meeting with the Director now, Kurt. I'm glad we had this chat. This lecture is going to do a lot of good for the School of Mathematics in many different ways. We will speak later."

⋮

Von Neumann made sure *everyone* in the Princeton and New York mathematical communities knew about the big lecture. He personally invited the most distinguished professors of logic, including Alonzo Church from Princeton, Sammy Eilenberg from Columbia, and, of course, his IAS colleague—and

Gödel's *bête noir*—Hermann Weyl. For his part, Gödel decided to focus his presentation on the famous Continuum Hypothesis, first enunciated by Georg Cantor in 1874. Following his work on mathmatical incompleteness, Gödel had devoted much of his mathematical effort to trying to settle this problem. Cantor's hypothesis had attracted so much attention that Hilbert had put it at the top of his list of 23 problems whose solution was important for the development of mathematics, which he presented in his historic address to the International Mathematical Congress in Paris in 1900.

The Continuum Hypothesis is about the existence of different levels of infinity. Starting with the style of infinity represented by the natural numbers 1, 2, 3, . . . , which is called *countably infinite* and denoted by the first letter of the Hebrew alphabet "$\aleph_0$" (aleph-zero), Cantor used an ingenious argument to show that the level of infinity represented by the real numbers was strictly greater than that of the natural numbers. The set of real numbers consists of all possible subsets of natural numbers. This is now termed the power of the *continuum* and is represented by the symbol "c." The Continuum Hypothesis states that there is no level of infinity that is strictly larger than $\aleph_0$ and smaller than c.

In 1938 Gödel showed that if you use the axioms of set theory and symbolic logic most familiar to working mathematicians, you cannot disprove the Continuum Hypothesis. In other words, the Continuum Hypothesis is consistent with these axioms. But he was never able to establish the converse,, namely, that you cannot prove it either, using this same axiomatic framework.

As news of Gödel's upcoming lecture spread throughout the local mathematical communities, a rumor arose that perhaps Gödel had finally succeeded in settling the second half of the problem to the effect that it was also not possible to prove the Continuum Hypothesis using this standard axiomatic framework. Because Gödel was notoriously reclusive and almost never gave lectures, this rumor acquired some currency. After all, why would the fanatically reclusive Gödel make a public presentation if he didn't have something extraordinary to announce? The buzz associated with this possibility pumped up interest in the lecture to almost feverish proportions before the day of the lecture arrived. As he stepped to the podium to introduce the talk, von Neumann realized that he had never seen the seminar room at the IAS School of Mathematics so crowded with curious onlookers. Absolutely *everyone* who was anyone was here.

"Distinguished colleagues and guests," he began. "Welcome to the School of Mathematics Colloquium. Nearly 20 years ago, our colleague, Kurt Gödel, obtained one of the most unexpected results in the history of mathematics—essentially, that deductive argumentation has inherent limitations for uncovering mathematical truth, even in the limited domain of the arithmetic of the natural numbers. In the intervening years, there has been much confusion and many differences of opinion on what these results *really* imply for our ability to settle every well-formulated mathematical proposition. Today, Kurt has generously offered to give us a brief account of his thoughts during the process of obtaining his results, and to present his personal opinion on these matters of mathematical philosophy. So I give the floor to him now for what I'm certain will be a fascinating and enlightening presentation."

Moving to the front of the lecture room, Gödel peered out at the audience through his thick, perfectly circular spectacles. He looked like someone who was caught in a spotlight and wondered why. Uh-oh, thought von Neumann, this is not a good beginning. The last thing he wanted was for Gödel to project the air of a confused, slightly mad professor. That would not help him argue Gödel's case for promotion at all.

Everyone in the audience, especially von Neumann,

began to get a bit uneasy at Gödel's seeming reluctance to begin the talk. But suddenly his eyes snapped into focus and he seemed to realize where he was and why. Gathering his thoughts, Gödel began to speak softly—but clearly and precisely—launching into some of the history of his celebrated work on incompleteness in arithmetic and his contribution to the solution of the Continuum Hypothesis.

"In March 1928 in Vienna, I attended two stimulating lectures by L.E.J. Brouwer, the famous Dutch topologist and logician. These lectures showed me what was known and what remained to be discovered in mathematical logic at that time. About one year later, I obtained a copy of Hilbert and Ackermann's book, *Grundzüge der theoretische Logik* (*The Foundations of Theoretical Logic*), in which they stated the problem of the completeness of predicate logic as an open problem. My doctoral dissertation settled this problem by showing that, indeed, predicate logic is complete; every valid statement one can make in predicate logic can be proved."

Here Gödel was referring to the form of logic that underlies all of set theory. First-order predicate calculus or first-order logic is a theory in symbolic logic that formalizes quantified statements such as "There exists an object with the property that . . ." or "For all objects, the following is true . . . ." First-order logic is distinguished from higher-order logic in that it does not allow statements such as "For every property, the following is true . . ." or "There exists a set of objects such that . . . ." Nevertheless, first-order logic is strong enough to formalize all of set theory and thereby virtually all of mathematics. It is the classical logical theory underlying mathematics.

Now entering into the spirit of his talk, Gödel roamed steadily back and forth across the front of the seminar room, as relentless in pursuit of his theme as a lion stalking its prey in the African savannah.

"But predicate logic is much too weak to deal with the

questions that most interest us—those involving the relationship between whole numbers, the realm of arithmetic. Then, one year after completing my dissertation, I discovered a way to code every statement about numbers into a number itself. This coding scheme allowed me to get arithmetic to, in effect, talk about itself. Thus, I was able to use numbers in both a syntactic and a semantic fashion. On the one hand, a given number was coded for some assertion about the relationship between numbers and thus had semantic content within arithmetic; on the other hand, that number was simply a number and, thus, had no real meaning beyond that fact. This dual character of numbers allowed me to create for any consistent logical system a number-theoretical statement that was undecidable—could not be proved or disproved—using that logical system."

By this, Gödel meant that he was able to translate the sentence, "This statement is unprovable" into a proposition about numbers. His coding scheme then provided a means to further translate this numerical proposition into a number itself. This number was then the "codeword" for an undecidable proposition, one that is provable if and only if it is not provable.

"As consistency of the logical framework was an indispensable condition for the incompleteness result to hold, I was always concerned about whether the particular system being employed could in some way actually prove its own consistency. This would have been quite a feat, akin somehow to pulling yourself up by your bootstraps. But by employing essentially the same lines of reasoning as for the incompleteness theorem, I was able to show that it is impossible for a logical system to prove its own consistency."

At this juncture someone from the audience asked if this meant that mathematics was always tentative, relying on assumptions like consistency that could never really be demonstrated, but only assumed. Gödel replied that he would address this kind of metamathematical question at the conclusion of his talk.

"Around 1930, I also ran across Hilbert's outline of a proposed proof of the Continuum Hypothesis. Sensitized to the metamathematical problems of arithmetic, I immediately saw the continuum problem as a question from the multiplication table of cardinal numbers (the positive integers, 1, 2, 3, . . .). The problem's intractability strongly suggested to me that the very notion of a *set* was in need of clarification. My own results on incompleteness and consistency had already pushed my thoughts in this direction, and the continuum problem only further convinced me that the right axioms of set theory had not yet been found."

Gödel went on to state that not only was the Continuum Hypothesis of interest in its own right, but that it served as a catalyst and testing ground for his ideas on what was the right concept of a set. By 1937 he had stated in private correspondence that he had succeeded in proving the consistency of the Continuum Hypothesis with the usual axioms of set theory, showing that the Hypothesis could not be disproved using this axiomatic framework. At that time he showed the outline of his proof only to von Neumann and Karl Menger, a Viennese colleague who was at that time professor at the University of Notre Dame in the United States. Gödel told the colloquium audience about this discovery.

"The first step in my proof was not to prove the Continuum Hypothesis directly, but to prove only its consistency with the axioms of set theory. Next, I wanted to use only definable properties of sets and relations instead of invoking recursive definitions that create an object by an infinite process. The final step in my argument is to take all ordinal numbers (roughly, the number of elements of a set of ordered numbers, for example, the ordinal number of the set $\{1, 2, 3, \ldots, n\}$

is n) as given rather than trying to construct them from first principles."

Hearing this last remark, von Neumann nodded his head benevolently and looked at the audience to see how many would join him in recognition of Gödel's resolutely Platonistic view of mathematics, in which objects like the ordinal numbers exist independent of the human mind or of any specific procedure for explicitly constructing them.

When he looked back to the front of the room, von Neumann was horrified to see Gödel facing the blackboard, scribbling some incomprehensible symbols, while muttering in a low voice that was totally inaudible to those in the room. Good God, thought von Neumann, this could turn into a first-class disaster if Gödel goes into his absent-minded professor act. If there was ever a time to be clear, direct, and communicative, it was now. Hoping to bring Gödel back to the land of the living, von Neumann interjected a question: "Kurt, could you say what the principal tool was that you used to obtain the consistency of the Continuum Hypothesis with the axioms of set theory?"

"Oh, yes. It was my creation of the notion of a *constructible set*."

"And what, precisely, is that?" continued von Neumann, hoping to draw out Gödel and have him explain to this audience of non-logicians what a magical rabbit he had pulled out of his mathematical hat to prove this extremely difficult result.

To von Neumann's dismay, Gödel turned again to the blackboard, saying, "The constructible sets are a specific example of a collection of sets that satisfy all the axioms of set theory, and with which the Continuum Hypothesis is consistent. Therefore, the Continuum Hypothesis cannot be disproved using the usual setup in logic, since it is consistent with the axioms. In the language of logicians, the constructible sets are a *model* for set theory."

At this juncture, Weyl interrupted Gödel to ask his view of the reality of mathematical objects. In particular, he asked if Gödel believed that a level of infinity between the integers and the real numbers truly *existed,* in the same sense that the seminar room or the piece of chalk Gödel was holding had an objective existence. Continuing to peer at the blackboard as if searching in the chalk dust for the perfect answer to this almost metaphysical question, Gödel finally began to expound his Platonistic view of mathematical objects.

"I believe that we do have objectivity in mathematics. Propositions about numbers are either true or false. Facts are independent of arbitrary conventions. And theorems about numbers characterize objective facts about integers. Moreover, these facts must have a content, because the consistency of number theory is derived from higher facts, and we can't assume any kind of set because if we did, number theory would not be consistent; we would get contradictions."

Carl Ludwig Siegel, one of the professors at the Institute who opposed Gödel's promotion, and a world-renowned number theorist himself, now stood up and in a booming voice overlaid with a heavy German accent, enquired, "So you do 'objective' mathematics? You feel that mathematicians discover objects rather than create them, much like the stars being there quite independently of the existence of astronomers to look at them?"

"Yes," said Gödel, finally turning away from the blackboard to face his interlocutor, "Mathematics is an empirical science. In my view the Continuum Hypothesis definitely has an answer—Yes or No. We have just not yet looked at the continuum hard enough to see what the answer is."

"Would you say, then," asked Weyl, "that the set of natural numbers has an independent existence that we can 'see,' in the same way, for instance, that we can look around Manhattan and see the Empire State Building?"

"Absolutely," Gödel shot back, in perhaps his most aggressive statement in the lecture. "Anyone who takes the trouble to learn a little mathematics can 'see' the set of natural numbers for himself. So the natural numbers must have an independent existence as a certain abstract possibility of thought."

One of the bright-eyed and bushy-tailed graduate students in logic who had come over from Princeton University to attend the seminar then asked naïvely, "What is the best way to perceive this pure abstract possibility?"

"First," replied Gödel, "you must close off the other senses, for example, by lying down in a quiet, darkened room. But this passive, rather negative action is by no means sufficient. You must actively seek with the mind. Do not forget that the mind is capable of perceiving infinite sets. So don't just imagine combinations and permutations of physical objects—finite things. Look to the infinite. The ultimate goal of such an exercise is to perceive the Absolute."

Oh no, thought von Neumann. Now Gödel has really gone too far. Veering off into what sounds like a lot of mystical mumbo-jumbo in front of this high-powered, mathematical audience, is not going to help me make a case to the faculty for his sanity and mathematical judgment. I must derail this line of discussion immediately and move things back to the purely mathematical. But before he could even open his mouth to redirect the discussion, the unrelenting Weyl was back.

"For myself, I believe that mathematics is mind-*dependent;* the objects of mathematics, such as a possible 'style' of infinity in between the integers and the reals, is not an objective fact but rather something that we must be able to construct. If we can, it exists; otherwise, it does not."

Gödel looked at Weyl in the same pitiless manner he might use to inspect some loathsome insect creeping from behind his refrigerator, before finally stating, "I will not argue with my esteemed colleague on this point. I simply state that although intuition represents a relationship between the human mind and mathematical reality, the mathematical world goes beyond our perception of it—just as the physical world does. This is what it means to be mind-independent."

The introduction of the world of tangible, physical objects into the discussion calmed von Neumann's growing concern at the metaphysical turn the discussion had been taking. He saw that the physicists in the crowd were now ready to join in, as Gödel's remark about our perception of the physical world set the antennae of the quantum theorists buzzing. The first to get his oar in the water was, interestingly enough, one of the youngest, the brilliant newcomer from England, Freeman Dyson, who spoke to Gödel but looked directly at von Neumann, as he said: "Your results prove that there are inherent limitations in every logical system. So regardless of the axiomatic framework we choose, there is some proposition that can be stated but neither proved nor disproved using the rules of that system. We quantum physicists also have a fundamental principle that constricts what we can know by measurement: the Heisenberg Uncertainty Principle, which limits how accurately we can simultaneously know the values of certain pairs of properties that a particle may possess, like position and momentum or time and energy. It's impossible not to speculate about whether these two types of limiting results—yours and Heisenberg's—have a common root. Or is it just a tempting analogy? Do you have any thoughts on this?"

Again von Neumann benevolently nodded his approval of Dyson's query, since it was precisely the kind of question he hoped someone would ask. There was little doubt in his mind that by linking Gödel's work to something as central to the scientific mindset in Princeton as Heisenberg uncertainty, the question would draw attention to the profundity of what Gödel had achieved. He squirmed in his seat, impatiently awaiting Gödel's reply. Finally, the Ruler of the Platonic

Realm spoke.

"It is very important to distinguish the world of mathematical objects from that of the physical. Both Heisenberg's result and my own are first and foremost mathematical results about mathematical objects. In Heisenberg's case, the objects are mathematical transformations [technically: operators] representing different properties that might be measured about a quantum object like an electron. The inherent uncertainty his principle asserts comes from comparing the measurement process for two different properties, such as position and momentum. If the order in which you carry out the measurement of this pair of properties makes no difference, then the corresponding operators commute and there is no inherent problem in simultaneously measuring both properties to arbitrary accuracy. But if the order does make a difference, the operators do not commute and there is an irremovable level of uncertainty in any such pair of measurements. This commutativity is a mathematical condition that can be checked for any two pairs of operators.

"It happens that we can correlate *approximately* these mathematical operators with physical properties, and then transfer the noncommutativity of a pair of such objects into an inherent limitation on how accurately we can measure the corresponding properties. But then you have passed from the mathematical to the physical, introducing a host of new questions surrounding the degree to which the idealized mathematical representation of the measurement situation corresponds to the actual physical setup in the laboratory."

Dyson, not to be put off by this basically mathematical reply, carried his question one step further.

"As a natural scientist, my interest is whether something akin to the limits you show for mathematics could ever arise in the world of real objects. This is why I ask about Heisenberg uncertainty. Every experiment ever performed confirms that we cannot simultaneously know the position and momentum of a particle to arbitrary accuracy. This appears to me to be a limit on what can be known, just as your incompleteness results show there are limits to what we can deduce by logical argument. Can you say something about these limitations on what can be known in the very different worlds of mathematical and physical objects?"

Before Gödel could open his mouth, a buzz of loud mutterings arose as several members of the audience attempted to join the discussion. One of the visitors from the Princeton University Physics Department shouted just a bit louder than the rest, asking Gödel his view of the truth of Euclidean geometry. Distracted from Dyson's question by the new direction this question led, Gödel seemed to go into a state of momentary paralysis, at which point von Neumann thought he had better step in and calm things down. Rising, he asked the audience to please conduct their questioning in a more orderly fashion, and allow Gödel to respond to one question before firing off another. This intercession seemed to offer just the breathing space Gödel needed to gather his thoughts and address the question about geometry.

"Geometrical intuition, strictly speaking, is not mathematical, but rather a priori physical intuition. In its purely mathematical aspect our Euclidean space intuition is perfectly correct; namely, it represents correctly a certain structure existing in the realm of mathematical objects. Even physically it is correct 'in the small,' that is, in the immediate neighborhood of a single point in space.

"But I want to emphasize that the congruence between the properties of mathematical objects such as points, lines, and planes and their real-world correlates is not a question of mathematics; it is more a question in the realm of mathematical epistemology or ontology, in which we investigate the relationship between the objects of the mathematical universe and those of the world of the natural sciences."

Von Neumann thought this was just the right moment to bring the proceedings to a close and stood up to thank the audience for their attention and lively discussion. In his closing remarks he said he thought Gödel's exposition had brought a deeper understanding of where the incompleteness results stood in the scientific scheme of things and hoped that the audience agreed with him.

After giving the customary round of applause for Gödel's presentation, the audience filed out of the seminar room, von Neumann and Weyl the last to go. As they left, von Neumann stopped Weyl in the corridor to ask him again about his views regarding Gödel's promotion.

"Hermann, I think Gödel's presentation this afternoon makes it obvious that his work plays a central role in our thinking about the relationship between mathematics and the world of matter and energy. As a mathematical physicist yourself, I'm sure you saw these connections long ago. So do you still oppose Gödel's promotion to Professor on the grounds that his incompleteness results are somehow dangerous for mathematics?"

"You know very well, Johnny, that my objections were never about the quality of Gödel's work. I do believe that his Platonistic view on the existence of mathematical objects is wrong-headed and sets mathematics onto an unhappy course, philosophically speaking anyway. But my real concerns over Gödel being a full professor are mostly about what I see as his otherworldly nature and, to put it bluntly, his mental instability. You know better than anyone that being a Professor at the IAS involves an enormous amount of administrative duty to keep the School of Mathematics alive and viable. Gödel's legalistic turn of mind could paralyze this entire process. That is my principal concern. And it is the same concern expressed by others in the School, including Siegel and Montgomery.

We simply must be confident that Gödel will not be a logjam in our procedures. Do you have any thoughts on how to deal with this problem?"

"To be honest, Hermann, I do not. But I will speak with others, as well as with Gödel himself, before the faculty meeting and see if there is some middle ground that everyone can feel comfortable with. As the meeting is more than two weeks away, let us try to talk again soon about this. Maybe by next week I'll have a solution to propose to you."

Chapter Five

THE BOARDROOM

J. Robert Oppenheimer sat slouched in his leather desk chair, necktie askew, staring out the window of the Director's corner office in Fuld Hall. He was considering the Institute for Advanced Study's (IAS) Board of Trustees meeting coming up later in the day, knowing that with von Neumann's computer project on the agenda, the meeting would be contentious. While some of the board members were in Johnny's corner, Oppenheimer knew he had to perform a delicate balancing act to avoid statements that would surely be leaked and would then alienate those faculty members opposed to the project. As Director of this band of overachieving intellects and socially unaware misfits, Oppenheimer realized he was caught right in the middle of this particular conflict. His mind raced through myriad strategies for resolving the conflict, discarding them one by one like a gambler throwing away low cards in a poker game. Oppenheimer ruminated on how this computer idea reached the IAS in the first place. As always, the central character in the story was von Neumann.

At the end of the war, the team of John W. Mauchly, J. Presper Eckert, Herman Goldstine, von Neumann, and others working on the Electronic Discrete Variable Computer (EDVAC) at the University of Pennsylvania's Moore School saw that the university was not going to continue supporting their work. Despite Penn's unchallenged technical virtuosity in computing technology, university administrators showed a lack of interest in retaining any of the participants except for von Neumann, who was never part of the Penn engineering faculty anyway but simply on leave from the IAS. Moreover, the Penn administration was keen to ensure that they retained the patent on any work done by their staff members, a policy that irritated both Eckert and Mauchly. With this writing all over the wall, they decided to form their own company to produce computing machines, a venture they hoped would be profitable. Von Neumann had another idea: He wanted his own computer, not to sell, but to use for scientific investigations.

After discussing the future of the computer project with Goldstine, von Neumann decided that future should be in Princeton—at the IAS, in fact. He felt that the environment there, together with the presence of the Radio Corporation of America (RCA) Laboratories down the road and the open intellectual climate in Princeton, was more conducive to his view of the computer as a tool for the entire scientific community than as a commercial device or one solely for the government and the military. That was when the trouble started, at least in the IAS intellectual hierarchy.

Von Neumann may have been the most productive IAS faculty member in terms of deploying his talents on behalf of the government during the war, but he certainly wasn't the only one. Even the great pacifist Einstein saw the need to resist the Axis powers and gave advice to the U.S. Navy on various questions in basic physics associated with naval operations. So, naturally, von Neumann thought that the faculty, even those residing in the rarefied heights of the School of Mathematics, would immediately see the virtues of having a computer close at hand and rubber-stamp his proposal for building one at the IAS. What a mistake! Clever men often have intellectual blind spots. And extremely clever men—perhaps those who are the cleverest of all—have the biggest blind spots when they depart from their areas of expertise. Von Neumann simply failed to understand the emotionally laden psyches of his colleagues. The chance to savor the pleasure of being employed at the IAS, where there are no students, no lectures, and no formal duties of any kind, attracts a very special type of intellect: the type that does not empathize with students, does not wish to be distracted by the mundane duties of giving lecture courses, and wants peace and quiet to contemplate its intellectual navel. Most especially, it attracts those who disdain mere "applications" of science as being a violation of the Platonic ideal to which they feel themselves—and the IAS—are dedicated.

So when von Neumann walked in and started lobbying the faculty for his computer project, the genius from Budapest was in for a shock. Not only did his sales pitch fall on deaf ears, in some cases it fell on manifestly hostile ones. And the expressions of hostility were definitely not *sotto voce*. The faculty was fundamentally opposed to such a venture on principle, as well as by precept. The IAS faculty was not about to sully itself by sanctioning an applied project if they could help it. And they could help it. Or so they thought. Von Neumann, a man who relished tackling only the most intractable and difficult of problems, thought otherwise. And therein lay Oppenheimer's dilemma.

The Director knew that the prestige of the IAS, and thus

its position in the pecking order of academia, rested entirely on the brilliance and reputation of its faculty. And among the faculty's many stars, only Einstein shone brighter than Johnny. He also knew that von Neumann could name his price—including the computer project—at any institution in the world, and get it. In fact, he had it on good authority that Robert Hutchins at the University of Chicago had approached von Neumann to join his radical experiment in education by bringing his brilliance and his computer to the Midwest. And local gossip had it that a similar overture had been made by the University of California. Oppenheimer had no illusions about Johnny's readiness to jump to one of these or to another more congenial environment with his project if the Institute's board turned down his proposal. Yes, he thought, this meeting is going to be *difficult*. And that's putting it mildly.

$$\vdots$$

Carl Ludwig Siegel, one of the finest—and most outspoken—mathematical analysts of the day, reflected on von Neumann's approach to him a few days earlier to enlist his support for building a computer on the hallowed grounds of the IAS. Siegel, a man brought up in the classical German tradition of scholarship, wondered how a computer might help his work.

A traditional mathematician like Siegel uses a lot of paper and pencil, chalk and blackboard, in trying out ways of putting abstruse symbols together into beautiful patterns. What kind of patterns look beautiful? Siegel would give the very same answer to this query as a poet, sculptor, or composer: A pattern that is pleasing to the intellect, expresses ideas in a compact manner, and is in some way surprising. So, for instance, Euler's formula $e^{\pi i} + 1 = 0$ is just such a beautiful pattern, displaying an entirely unexpected relationship between the five most important constants in mathematics: 0, 1, e (the base of natural logarithms), π (the ratio of a circle's circumference to its diameter), and i (the square root of -1, which forms the basis for the complex numbers). Siegel didn't think having a computer would have helped Euler one bit in discovering this remarkable formula. Nor did he think a machine that could compute a table of logarithms or add up a long column of numbers would help his own work any more than a lathe in a metal-working shop would help a metal sculptor create a beautiful piece for his garden. The lathe might be a useful tool in *shaping* some metal for such a sculpture, Siegel conceded, but it certainly was not any more necessary for creating the vision embodied in the work than was the pencil he was presently using to jot down Euler's formula on the piece of paper on his desk.

Siegel also objected to von Neumann's project on aesthetic grounds. He recalled seeing a message while serving in the German army at the western front in the First World War that read, "Cavalry officers entering balloons are required to remove their spurs." A sharp-edged, *applied* project like von Neumann's had no more business at a place like the IAS than did spurs in a balloon. The IAS was dedicated to the exploration of the limits of the human intellect. It just wasn't right to be building mere machines at such a place. The Institute was an *idea incubator,* not a factory for cranking out ideas in a mechanical manner like a meat-processing plant spitting out sausages. No, Carl Ludwig Siegel would certainly not vote to open the Institute to such a venture. Not even his boundless respect for von Neumann's intellect would allow him to go quite that far. In fact, he thought—and sometimes even stated, in private—that von Neumann was wasting his enormous talents on such a quixotic quest as the construction of a computing machine.

But among the mathematicians, von Neumann's computer project had its supporters, too.

Herrontown Woods, just outside Princeton, is one of the greenest and loveliest tracts of land for miles in any direction, the perfect place for getting away from the noise and stench of motor cars to hike or just sit and think quietly. At the very moment Siegel was sitting at a desk in Fuld Hall contemplating von Neumann and his computer, one of the project's staunchest supporters was enjoying these woods as he mulled over his view of that very same exalted personage and project. Oswald Veblen, a tall, slim Scandinavian-looking man, was one of the leaders of the American mathematical community. A nephew of the famed economist and social theorist Thorstein Veblen, author of *The Theory of the Leisure Class,* Veblen was known worldwide for his pioneering work in geometry and topology. He and Einstein were the first two professors recruited to the IAS in 1932 by its founding Director, Abraham Flexner. Before then Veblen had been head of the Mathematics Department at Princeton University, to which he had invited von Neumann as a visiting faculty member in 1930. When the IAS was founded a couple of years later, Veblen convinced Flexner to appoint von Neumann as the youngest permanent Professor, and he thereafter regarded von Neumann almost as the son he had never had.

At one of the IAS mathematics faculty meetings, Veblen took notes on the discussion surrounding the computer project. After detailing Siegel's objections and Marston Morse's less than enthusiastic remark to the effect that, while the project seemed inevitable, it was very far from desirable, Veblen noted in his characteristic self-deprecatory fashion that he simple-mindedly welcomed the advance of science in whatever direction it might go. So von Neumann could certainly count on the support of this ultrarespectable and enormously influential faculty member. The computer project certainly had its advocates, and powerful ones, too; no doubt about that.

Veblen was already head of the Mathematics Department when Fine Hall was built on the Princeton University campus to house the mathematicians. Reflecting his collegial view of mathematical practice, he had the Commons Room placed so that everyone had to pass it to get to the library, reasoning that this proximity would increase the solidarity of the mathematics faculty and students. So no one was surprised when Veblen, with his collaborative view of how mathematics should be done, used his great prestige to try to heal the intellectual rifts generated between von Neumann and some of the more unreconstructed members of the IAS faculty by the proposed computer project. In fact, though, everyone loved Johnny. Some just didn't love his computer idea.

⋮

Reserve Admiral Lewis L. Strauss, partner in the New York investment firm of Kuhn, Loeb & Company, sprawled across the back seat of his chauffered car as it moved along the highway to Princeton for the IAS Board of Trustees meeting that afternoon. Strauss ignored the oil refineries dotting the bleak New Jersey flatlands, focusing instead on the fight he anticipated in the boardroom later. He was a trim man of medium height—but with a short man's personality: pugnacious and combative. He was also a man of practical action and movement, who harbored a deep suspicion of most academics, whom he regarded as dreamers. As his thoughts moved to the Institute's Director, Oppenheimer, Strauss's eyes narrowed and his mouth turned down into a grimace, thinking about the enormous mistake the trustees had made in naming such a man to head the IAS. Oppenheimer was brilliant, yes, but unstable and, even worse, politically unreliable, in Strauss's opinion. One might make a case for having Oppenheimer on the faculty. But Director? Never!

Strauss's normally stern features softened considerably, though, as he shifted attention to the agenda for the meeting, noting that the very first item was consideration of Johnny von Neumann's computer project. Now here was a man to admire, he thought. Not only the most brilliant scientist of his generation, but a man who saw the world in its proper light. And the hue of that light was definitely not the red of the Soviet Union! In Strauss's world the red-white-and-blue of the U.S.A. was the only acceptable color scheme. If there was one thing the ultraconservative Strauss knew, it was that. And it infuriated him no end that at the IAS, from the Director on down, von Neumann was the only scientist at this glorified home for wayward intellectuals who saw things clearly.

As a nonscientist himself, but a banker and financier, Strauss had a not unusual tendency among businessmen to admire successful scientists. People like von Neumann and Einstein resided somewhere in his pantheon of heroes, although he had residual negative feelings about Einstein from their conversations when the trustees were selecting a Director. When Strauss queried Einstein on the type of man he thought should be chosen, the great physicist said he would prefer someone quiet who wouldn't disturb people while they were thinking. Well and good, agreed Strauss. But when their conversation turned to the candidacy of Oppenheimer, whose left-leaning political views overlapped considerably with Einstein's own, Strauss simply could not understand how a genius like Einstein could fail to see the completely obvious menace posed by the Soviet Union. Too many years hunched over the books, he finally concluded, and not enough contact with everyday reality. This was just the kind of otherwordly attitude that Strauss found most disturbing about the IAS. But at today's meeting he would at least have the chance to strike a blow for something practical and useful when the computer project came up for consideration. Anything von Neumann wanted to do had to be worth doing, and as an IAS trustee he felt an obligation to use his influence to strongly support any such proposal.

The car pulled up to the entrance to Fuld Hall, and as the driver came around the car and opened the door, Strauss shot out of the back seat as if he'd been fired from a cannon. In the Institute's foyer, he nearly had a head-on collision with his *bête noire,* Oppenheimer, who was just leaving his office on his way to the meeting. Grabbing onto Oppenheimer to keep him from toppling, Strauss greeted the Director with sugar on his tongue but murder in his heart, before walking with him into the large oak-paneled conference room where the rest of the board was already assembled. The deep-pile carpeting, English hunting prints on the wall, and heavy velvet drapes pulled across the windows all reminded Strauss of a boardroom in his usual Wall Street haunts. He felt comfortable and was clearly energized and ready to fight the good fight against the pointy-headed academics standing in the way of his hero's noble venture.

As Oppenheimer and Strauss took their seats—at opposite ends of the oversized mahogany table—the chairman of the board, a rather formidable lawyer from Philadelphia, opened the meeting. After the standard formalities of reading and approving the minutes from the last meeting, the Chairman turned to the first—and what turned out to be the only—item on the agenda that day: von Neumann's computer project.

"Gentlemen," the chairman intoned in a stentorian, get-the-attention-of-the-jury voice, "the first item on our agenda today is to consider Professor von Neumann's proposal to construct a computing machine here at the IAS. As you all know, there is considerable division on the faculty as to the desirability of this venture. Perhaps it's best if Director Oppenheimer quickly summarizes the situation as it stands today. Oppie?"

Looking up at the group from his seat, Oppenheimer quickly sketched the faculty's principal objection to the project.

"Those on the faculty opposed to this project are quite vocal about it. They feel that the very essence of what the IAS stands for is thinking of the most rarefied kind. In their view this is what sets the IAS apart from a university, an industrial research center, or a government laboratory. The role model for this 'Platonic heaven' is Plato's Academy in ancient Athens, where would-be scholars met to study abstract subjects such as philosophy and mathematics at the feet of masters like Plato himself. It is hardly a surprise, then, that those holding this view of the Institute's *raison d'être* are opposed to a project they regard as mere engineering, an applied venture having no place in such an intellectual environment. Of course, there are those on the faculty who are indifferent to the project. However, I feel compelled to add that with the exception of Professor von Neumann himself, there are no members of the School of Mathematics who are genuinely enthusiastic about it. It is my understanding, though, that Professor Veblen supports the project. But that support seems more for the sake of keeping von Neumann in Princeton than for the computer itself. And that is where we stand at the moment."

The board sat silent for a moment digesting Oppenheimer's summary. A wooden ceiling fan turned slowly, keeping pace with their thoughts as they pondered this dilemma. Should they turn down von Neumann and thereby run the risk that this most visible member of the faculty might leave for greener pastures? Would this be tantamount to siding with the Old Guard and voting to preserve the status quo, endorsing the traditional image of the IAS as a scholarly refuge in the true Platonic mold? Or could there possibly be some course between von Neumann and the traditionalists that would give half a loaf to each side? Before any debate had a chance to begin, Oppenheimer offered a suggestion.

"I think the position of the anti-computer faction is quite clear and needs no further elaboration. But I know that many of you are not fully aware of Professor von Neumann's vision of what the computer means to the practice of science and why he feels so strongly that the IAS is the right place to build it. So if there are no objections, I've asked him to come to the meeting today and give us all a brief summary of his views and the scope of the project he has in mind."

Looking around the room, Oppenheimer saw several trustees glancing at each other and nodding their heads in agreement. Of course, Oppenheimer knew that except for himself, Johnny was the best person in the Institute to explain an idea in terms that a nonspecialist could understand. His ploy to get von Neumann to the podium was calculated to muster as much ammunition as he could in support of the project—without being seen to be taking sides. "As I hear no objections, let me call Professor von Neumann into the room."

As Oppenheimer left the room to fetch von Neumann, the trustee next to Strauss leaned over and whispered, "I've heard von Neumann is an even greater genius than Einstein. How can the IAS be debating about whether to do this project? It seems to me that the very essence of a Platonic heaven like this one is that the professors should be able to follow whatever intellectual interests they wish. Otherwise, what's the point of a place like the IAS?"

Strauss nodded vigorously in agreement. Just then Oppenheimer reentered the room, followed by the roly-poly figure of von Neumann, dressed for success as always in a well-cut, medium-gray, three-piece banker's suit, conservative maroon necktie, and highly polished, black, wing-tip shoes. Just the costume to make these lawyers, bankers, and high-level academics feel at ease with one of their own. Stepping up to the front of the room with a bounce in his step and a smile on his cherubic face, von Neumann looked like nothing so much as a friendly carnival pitchman or perhaps an upmarket salesman for an expensive brand of automobile, such as the Cadillacs he was so fond of himself. He began by recounting the historical connection between advances in technology and advances in scientific knowledge.

"Gentlemen. Thank you very much for allowing me the time to present to you my thoughts on computing machines and their role in the future of science. Let me begin by just noting two historical examples of how technology and science go hand in hand. The first is Galileo's dramatic exploitation of the telescope to study the moons of Jupiter in 1609. My second example is Christiaan Huygens's construction of the microscope. Both inventions amplified the power of the human eye to see farther and deeper into the structure of matter and the universe than ever before. The galactic pattern forming the universe and the cellular structure of living organisms are but two discoveries brought about by technological advances that have changed our view of ourselves and the world we live in. The computing machine will open up vistas far greater than even these examples, I promise you."

With the sense of timing of a good straight man in a comedy routine, Strauss immediately spoke up. "Tell me, please, Johnny, how you can be so sure of this? After all, a computing machine is simply a device for doing arithmetic, essentially addition, faster than any human brain can do it—other than perhaps yours." This last remark brought a smile to the faces of several board members familiar with von Neumann's legendary skill at mental arithmetic. "How does doing addition help us see the world differently?"

And just like a comedian whose straight man had fed him the right opening, von Neumann delivered the punch line. "Because the computer amplifies the power of the human mind to see further and further into the secrets of nature."

Now everyone was paying attention. How could a device that simply added numbers extend the power of the human mind? What is von Neumann playing at here? thought some. Even these sophisticated, educated professionals had the same, almost religious, view of the human mind clung to by the man on the street. The human mind is ineffable; it's something mysterious, bordering on the spiritual, and what could adding numbers have to do with that? Finally, the chairman voiced the question that was on everyone's mind.

"Dr. von Neumann. We all see that the human mind does arithmetic. That's clear. It's equally clear that your computer will be able to do calculations far faster and with greater reliability than any human could hope to achieve. But how can you claim that doing sums is tantamount to seeing deeper into the structure of the world around us? It may well be useful for bookkeeping, accounting for electricity bills, or even calculating important numbers like π to many digits. But this seems very far removed from the type of grand claims you are making for looking—what is your phrase?—'further and further' into nature."

"I agree," said one of the other trustees in a booming voice. "The mind certainly seems to be something more than a computing machine for calculating numbers."

Von Neumann hesitated momentarily and turned to the chalkboard on the wall behind him, seeming to mumble something that sounded like "nebbishes" under his breath. But no one in the room could really make out what he was saying, so they simply awaited his reply. Finally, he turned back to his audience.

"Let me give you an extremely simple example. Suppose you have five people who together possess ten dollars. I ask you: What is the average amount of money each person has? If I let x denote the average amount, and then multiply this quantity by the total number of people, I arrive at the total amount of money, which is ten dollars."

Turning to the chalkboard behind him, von Neumann

wrote on the board: $5x = 10$. "Here is a simple equation expressing in mathematical language what I've just told you in words. The answer to the real-world question about the average amount of money is the unknown in the equation, x. Solving for this quantity involves one division, which yields the answer that the average amount of money possessed by each person is x equals 2 dollars."

The chairman again intervened: "What is the point here, Dr. von Neumann? We can all see this."

"The point, Mr. Chairman, is that to answer this admittedly trivial real-world question, I had to carry out a calculation. I had to solve an equation for x, which in this ultra-elementary situation required a single division; or what is the same thing, several subtractions. *That* is the point. Solving problems about the real world always involves carrying out computations. So the better you are able to compute, the deeper you can penetrate into the world of nature and human beings."

At this point one of the other board members, a tired-looking man in a rumpled brown suit who almost never said anything at these meetings, raised his hand rather timidly. Von Neumann thought the man looked like an accountant, and cringed at the thought of what this little mouse of a man might ask. As fortune would have it, however, no one else was saying anything at that particular moment and von Neumann could not ignore the raised hand. To everyone's surprise, the question turned out to be crucial and dictated the course of the rest of the meeting.

"Well, it seems pretty obvious that scientific knowledge is somehow intimately tied up with solving equations," said the trustee. "But as far as I'm aware, scientists and mathematicians have been solving equations for a very long time. Hundreds of years, it seems. So what new element is your computer going to bring to this process? How is it going to change the way science is carried out? Besides, when I see an equation on a blackboard saying '*x* is a planet,' I don't see a planet; I see a *symbol* for a planet. I thought science was about matter, energy, things. You seem to be saying it's about mathematical 'pictures' of things. Can you clarify what you mean here?"

Ah, thought von Neumann. So there *is* a reason this man is on the board, after all. An enquiring brain really does reside beneath that plain, rather dim-looking exterior. Finally, we come to the essence of the matter. Johnny recalled the heated discussion of this very issue of the physical world versus the mathematical one at his party just a couple of nights earlier. So he was well sensitized to the distinction and eager to present to the board his arguments for how it related to the computer project.

"Give the gentleman a cigar," he said with a big smile. "This distinction between the physical world and the world of symbols and relations is one of the most important in all of philosophy. And it is mirrored perfectly in the computer. On the one hand, we have a physical device made of metal, glass, and other things, with electrical energy flowing through it in a particular way. Looked at from this perspective, the computer is indeed a piece of engineering, just as many of its IAS opponents claim. But there is another side to the story. And it is this side that supports its construction right here in this scholar's paradise."

Von Neumann could see Oppenheimer nodding enthusiastically, already far into the argument that was unfolding. Oppie knew the computer was not about matter and energy at all, but about *information*. It was the symbols and their relations to each other that counted, not the physical device that instantiated them. But how to explain this to the board so that it made practical, everyday sense? That was his mission. And he'd have to do it perfectly right now if he wanted their support for the project.

"The computer is just a physical device for housing a large number of electrical switches, each of which can be in one of two positions, ON or OFF, at any given moment. It is this ON–OFF *pattern* of the switches and how that pattern changes from moment to moment that determines what the computer is calculating. The pattern and the rule for changing the pattern are not matter or energy, they are pure information. In that sense, the computer's ON–OFF pattern is completely analogous to my writing the symbol x here on the blackboard, asking you to think of it as representing something in the real world. It is just a symbol, not the real thing, just as a map is not the physical territory. But we can use such symbols and rules for transforming sets of symbols into other sets to represent relationships in the real world.

"The computer can process sets of symbols and make and break patterns faster and more reliably than any device in the history of mankind. *That* is why this machine should be built at the IAS! Not because it is a piece of avant-garde engineering, but because it is the beginning of the replacement of matter and energy by information as the focal point of science."

"That's an extraordinary statement, Dr. von Neumann," asserted Strauss. "Can you justify it by a serious real-world example, not a schoolbook illustration in arithmetic like before?"

Von Neumann knew Admiral Strauss was setting him up to provide the *pièce de résistance* to the entire presentation, since he and Strauss had already spoken extensively about the great interest of the military, especially the U.S. Navy, in the development of computing machines. So when he walked into the room von Neumann had expected just this type of question from Strauss and was ready with his answer.

"Certainly. I think we all agree that a problem of enormous personal and economic interest to everyone is prediction of the weather. The old saying that 'Everyone talks about the weather, but no one does anything about it' reflects a commonly held view that prediction and control of the weather and other atmospheric phenomena are simply beyond our ability. That is definitely true—at the moment. And the biggest single obstacle is that we just do not understand enough about how different atmospheric processes interact with each other to produce what we call 'the weather.' The computing capability embodied in the type of machine I'm proposing will change all this."

Von Neumann went on to describe how the movement of fluids like air and water vapor and the transport of heat from one part of the earth to another are governed by a relationship described mathematically by the so-called Navier-Stokes equations. He told the board that unlike the simple arithmetic problem he had given earlier, there is no way to express the solution of these equations in terms of simple functions like exponentials, sines, cosines, or polynomials; the solution to the Navier-Stokes equations must be computed numerically. What this entails is a division of the earth's atmosphere into many little "boxes," and then solving for the numerical value of quantities like pressure, temperature, humidity, and so forth in each box at every moment in time. He went on to say that for such values to be useful in forecasting, hence understanding and controlling the weather, these values must be produced much faster than they actually unfold in nature. Calculating a prediction of tomorrow's weather the day after tomorrow would clearly be useless.

"All right. Now I see the connection with the computer," said the Chairman in an almost excited voice. "You need to do a very large number of calculations to obtain these values, and you have to do them fast."

"Indeed. Far faster than even an army of humans with hand calculating machines could ever hope to do. And they have to be carried out with very high precision, since the equations describing these atmospheric processes are very sensitive to small changes in the numbers characterizing the starting state of the atmosphere when the calculation begins.

"Let me add that weather prediction and control constitute only one of many critical problems in everyday life that we cannot effectively address by traditional mathmatical equations. And for the very same reason that the solution of these equations cannot be obtained in terms of elementary functions like polynomials, exponentials and the like: We have to compute them."

"What kinds of problems are these, Johnny?" asked Oppenheimer, again setting him up with a question calculated to impress upon the board the importance of the computer.

"Management of the national economy immediately comes to mind," shot back von Neumann. "It involves knowing about demands for goods and services, production capacity of firms, availability of workers, interest rates, and many other things that are continually changing over time. All these quantities are linked in equations that again can be solved only numerically. So the situation with economics is the same as with the weather. We need to carry out large volumes of calculations quickly to get the answers to the questions we most care about answering."

"So," said Strauss, "I think we can see why you say that scientific knowledge is limited by our ability to do calculations. Most, or at least many, of the problems in modern life do not have nice, neat, mathematical solutions; they require us to calculate numbers. And your computer is the quintessential calculator."

Von Neumann smiled at Strauss's summary before stating, "Precisely. And this is why I feel so strongly about constructing this machine here at the IAS. If it were built in a government laboratory or a corporate research center, the calculating power of the machine would be given over to uses peculiar to those organizations. In particular, many scientists in the academic world would never have access to the machine to further their investigations. I believe it is very important to be able to plan such a machine without any inhibitions, and to run it quite freely and governed only by scientific considerations. Building the machine here at the IAS will allow it to be available for general scientific work. Openness and accessibility are critical for the healthy development of science. And I think we all agree that that is why the IAS exists—to further the progress of knowledge by whatever means."

"And how much do you think it will cost to construct this machine?" asked Strauss, knowing that he was in a position to direct funds to the IAS to help this effort.

"I estimate the cost at about $400,000. This is for both the materials, which are very special in some instances, and scientific and engineering personnel to design and construct the machine. Let me add that I have already received assurances from RCA that they will contribute $100,000 as well as engineering support to build some very special-purpose electronics needed for the machine."

Sensing that the mutual admiration between Strauss and von Neumann was becoming a bit too obvious, the Chairman quickly moved to end the presentation and return the board to its deliberation on the computing project—without further input from Dr. von Neumann.

"I believe the board now has a much better sense of the potential of your project, Dr. von Neumann, as well as the way you see it fitting into the general scheme of things here at the IAS. We thank you very much for this enlightening presentation. Now I think we need to deliberate further on the matter. Dr. Oppenheimer will discuss our deliberations with you later."

Looking each board member in the eye for a moment, von Neumann quickly responded: "I thank you, as well, Mr.

Chairman. I trust the collective wisdom of the board to produce a wise decision on this proposal. I wish you all a good day." And with that the portly von Neumann stepped remarkably nimbly from the room, closing the door softly as he left.

⋮

As the door closed behind von Neumann, the chairman peered out at the board over his half-moon spectacles as if asking for someone, anyone, to start the discussion of what to do about this computer project. Surprisingly, it was the accountant from nowhere who spoke up first.

"I think Dr. von Neumann's project should be supported here at the IAS. In fact, I believe we should allocate money from the discretionary fund to help make it happen here. This is the most exciting activity I've heard about here in Princeton since I've been on this board. This Institute needs *more* avant-garde ideas like this and a lot less polishing of the existing scientific apple to a brighter shine."

This opening salvo energized the group and suddenly everyone wanted to speak. The chairman slapped the table and asked for a bit of decorum and order before giving the floor to Oppenheimer. As a kind of closet supporter of the computer project, Oppie had the opening he was waiting for to try to pound the last nail into the coffin of the project's detractors—but without putting himself on the record as doing so. Standing up to give a bit more authority to his statement, Oppenheimer declared:

"There is clearly much merit in what Dr. von Neumann is proposing. The computer is certainly a tool that will advance human knowledge in many important—and most likely unpredictable—ways. Generally speaking, that is indeed the mission of the IAS. So in that sense I heartily endorse the project. But as Director I must caution the board that we have a duty to consider as well the morale of the Institute faculty. The lifeblood of any institution is its people. And there are those here who strongly oppose this project. So I urge the board to take *all* these factors into account in coming to its decision."

From the tone of Oppenheimer's voice, his general demeanor, and the determined look in his eye, there was little doubt in anyone's mind as to where his heart and mind stood on the matter of the computing project. Yet his words held a measure of solace and empathy for those faculty who tenaciously clung to a more classical, less edge-of-the-frontier view of knowledge and its creation. As the last words left Oppenheimer's lips, Admiral Strauss decided to try and finish off the discussion on his terms, even though he personally loathed supporting anything that Oppenheimer endorsed. But for Johnny von Neumann he would make an exception.

"If the board will allow me, I would like to propose the following resolution of this question. Dr. von Neumann has said he has promises of substantial support from several sources in industry and government. Perhaps we might propose that if at least some of this support indeed materializes, the IAS will also contribute to the project as a kind of inducement to von Neumann to raise the rest of the money from outside sources. If he is able to do this, the Institute will then also agree to house the project."

One of the more silent board members, a businessman from somewhere in Pennsylvania, finally spoke up. "That sounds like a workable plan to me, since it places the burden for financing the project on von Neumann's shoulders. If he succeeds, it ensures that funding will come to the Institute at least to the level of covering all expenses—including von Neumann's salary. This should free up money to pay for additional faculty or visitors for the School of Mathematics, which in turn might mollify those faculty most opposed to this venture. Let me suggest additionally that the Director arrange to house this project in a separate structure, away from Fuld Hall, so the other faculty are not continually reminded of its existence."

Oppenheimer saw that things were going in exactly the direction he wished, and so stepped in quickly to try to get a general accord on this proposal before someone spoke against it.

"I see that it's already coming up onto 5 o'clock and I know that many of you still have long trips back to your homes. So let us hold over the remaining items on the agenda to our next meeting. I wish now to formally move that we accept the proposal just made: That the IAS agree to house this project and provide limited Institute funds to support it—provided Dr. von Neumann raises the rest of the costs beforehand from outside agencies."

Strauss immediately seconded the motion. The chairman looked around the room, his eyebrows raised in invitation to any dissenters. No objections being raised, he called for a vote. "All in favor?" A uniform chorus of "Ayes" adjourned the meeting.

Chapter Six

LATE-NIGHT THOUGHTS OF THE GREATEST PHYSICIST

The light from the upstairs corner room at the back cast a soft, yellowish glow on the backyard of the white clapboard house at 112 Mercer Street. At 11 o'clock on a late-spring evening the normal flow of traffic on this fairly busy residential street slowed considerably, making the neighborhood a good place for quiet contemplation. And that was exactly what the saintly looking white-haired gentleman in the rumpled dark-blue sweater sitting in the corner room was doing, as he leaned back and stared at the reflection of the desk lamp in the window. At the moment he was contemplating with nostalgic satisfaction the year 1905, which in the world of science had come to be known as the *annus mirabilis,* the year of miracles. Albert Einstein was thinking of the strange path his life had taken over nearly half a century, from his position as an examiner at the Swiss Patent Office in Berne in that year, to this study on Mercer Street today.

In that one unbelievable year, Einstein had published five articles in the journal *Annalen der Physik,* three of which pioneered three entirely new branches of physics, one of these papers being the surface reason quoted by the Nobel committee when they awarded him the prize in physics 18 years later, namely, the photoelectric effect, another of the papers being the one that began the theory of relativity. Very likely no physicist will ever again approach this feat. And this outpouring of genius sprang from a complete outsider to the profession, a mere patent examiner in a small town in Switzerland. Even Hollywood would turn down this story as being literally "incredible." And the most incredible part is that the man to whom it had happened was now nearly a complete outcast from the very community of physicists that had considered him their standard bearer and intellectual leader. What a wry cosmic joke, he thought. Having rebelled against authority his entire life, he was now paying for these sins by being an authority himself!

But the greatest scientist since Newton, and certainly the one scientist everyone in the world would recognize on sight, was now totally stumped. And he had been stumped for more than 20 years. His greatest creation, the general theory of relativity, linked space, time, and matter into one seamless theory—for *macro*scopic-sized objects like planets and galaxies. Yet just a few years later, an equally compelling theory of *micro*scopic-sized objects, electrons and photons and other fundamental particles—the quantum theory—burst onto the intellectual scene, in large part also due to Einstein's work. Unlike relativity theory, quantum theory was resolutely statistical. Electrons have only a certain *likelihood* of being found in a particular location until a measurement of their position is taken. General relativity, on the other hand, was purely classical; that is, objects moved in accordance with the rigidly deterministic laws of Newtonian mechanics. It was a completely consistent theory of the gravitational field. The quantum theory, however, gave a full account of light, hence was a theory of the electromagnetic field. How to bring these two fundamentally different sets of phenomena—gravity and electromagnetism—together into a single coherent theory, the unified field theory. That was the Holy Grail to which he had dedicated the past two decades of his life.

To make matters even worse in Einstein's view, the standard interpretation of the quantum theory postulated that observable quantities themselves, such as energy, momentum, and even time, are somehow created through the very process of observation and do not have an existence independent of who or what is doing the observing. A physicist of the old school, Einstein simply could not accept a Nature that was so capricious. "God is subtle," he often said, "but he is not malicious." The quantum theory must somehow be fundamentally incomplete, he thought. Another part of his job as a physicist was to find the holes in the theory—and plug them.

Staring at the paper on his desk, covered with arcane mathematical scribbles that only a mathematician or theoretical physicist could love, he angrily swept it aside as yet another blind alley in his Sisyphean quest for the elusive unified field. Yet once more he leaned back in his chair and wondered: Could Nature be *so* subtle and deep that it is really beyond the power of the primitive human brain to ever truly understand it? Is the scheme of Nature too complex in some fundamental way for the monkey brain we have inherited to fully comprehend its workings? But Einstein thought that to fall into such a belief is to concede the game before the first point is even played. Staring absently at the book-covered wall of his study and the clutter on his desk, he reached for the tobacco tin and began stuffing his pipe as he pondered the thought experiment he had concocted with Nathan Rosen and Boris Podolsky more than a decade ago to focus on the inherent inconsistencies of the mysterious quantum.

A naïve realist at heart, Einstein clung to the classical view that a particle, be it a billiard ball, a planet, or an electron, had well-defined properties like position and momentum at every single moment. *Au contraire,* said the quantum theorists from Copenhagen, Paris, Brussels, and Berlin. The very idea of a well-defined position at all times is an illusion stemming from an overdose of experience with macroscopic-sized objects like planets, tables, and chairs. In the microscopic realm of the quantum, an object like an electron has *no* properties whatsoever until it is actually observed. Then it acquires a position, a spin, or a momentum, depending on the nature of the measurement. So in an ontological sense, the properties are brought into existence by the act of measurement, by an observation.

Even worse, thought Einstein, the conventional wisdom of the quantum theorist is that before a measurement is made, all one can say about a property like the position of a particle such as an electron is that there is a certain probability that the electron will be found in such-and-such a location when the measurement is actually taken. One can say no more. In short, Nature is statistical, not deterministic. We can speak only of the likelihood of an event, not its certainty. I'll go to my grave, Einstein thought, resisting such a view of Nature. If this is the best that quantum theory can offer to explain the deep reality of the material world, then the theory must be fundamentally incomplete. Somewhere, somehow, the theory must be completed. Then all this nonsense about probabilities, unobserved particles, and so forth will vanish just like the mythical luminiferous aether, he believed. There must be hidden variables that the theory does not include, but whose values enable us to speak with certainty about properties of particles—even when no one is looking.

So what can one *really* know about an electron? Are the limits imposed by Heisenberg's Uncertainty Principle true limits built into the fabric of Nature? Or are they simply limits imposed by an incomplete theory, having nothing whatsoever to do with the way Nature is truly put together? Einstein, with his collaborators Rosen and Podolsky, created an experiment to bring this "limits" question into sharper focus.

Suppose, they said, you have a particle system composed of two electrons, with opposite spins, UP and DOWN, say. Then the total spin of the overall system is zero. Now, according to the quantum theorists from Copenhagen like Niels Bohr and Werner Heisenberg, neither electron can be said to have a definite spin, UP or DOWN, until it is measured, at which moment it immediately *acquires* one spin or the other. Before the measurement forces an UP or DOWN spin on it, the electron is in a nether state without either spin.

So, said Einstein and his collaborators, without having first determined the spin of either electron by observing it, let one of them be transported to the other side of the galaxy. Once it reaches its destination, let that electron's spin be measured by an observer. Suppose that measurement gives the spin as UP. Since the total spin in the system must be zero, then at the very instant you measure UP on the "traveling" electron, you immediately know—without making a measurement— that the stay-at-home electron's spin is DOWN. In fact, if you do then measure the stay-at-home electron's spin, you will unfailingly observe that it's spin *is* DOWN. So you have acquired knowledge of the stationary electron's spin without any measurement at all! This is the paradox. How did that information get across the galaxy so fast? Faster than the speed of light, actually, if the spin DOWN was not already inherent in the stationary electron. This was the puzzle that Einstein, Podolsky, and Rosen (EPR) posed to the quantum theorists.

The EPR paper divided the community of physicists into two camps: The first group is bothered by EPR. The second group is not, but is also divided into two subgroups. The first subgroup explains why it is not bothered, although the explanations tend to miss the point of EPR entirely or contain physical assertions that can be shown to be completely false. The other subgroup does not explain why it is not bothered; it just isn't. Some in this group claim that Einstein's close friend and debating partner, Niels Bohr, settled the whole thing— but they're not entirely sure how.

Ja, Einstein thought. Our idea really set the cat among the pigeons. Once those two electrons are "entangled" with opposite spins using the very rules the quantum theorists advocate, the problems start. After all, he argued to himself, if, without in any way disturbing the system of electrons it is possible to predict with certainty the value of the spin, then there exists an element of physical reality corresponding to the spin. In other words, if it's possible to deduce the spin of one particle by measuring the spin of its twin, both spins must already exist as elements of reality. Einstein then recalled how the original EPR paper used the properties of position and momentum instead of spin, which was a refinement introduced recently by the very clever young physicist David Bohm. But in either case, the idea of being able to know with certainty the state of one electron by measuring the state of the other is a total violation of Heisenberg's Uncertainty Principle, the bedrock upon which quantum theory rests. There simply *must* be something wrong with this theory! Einstein shouted silently to himself for the thousandth time.

Fortuitously, perhaps, at that very moment his thoughts were diverted from this negative turn by a soft knock on his study door. "*Komm,*" he said softly, as the door opened, revealing his wife, Elsa, with a tray in her hand. Remaining in the doorway—since it was a long-standing rule in the Einstein household that no one, but no one, ever entered his study—Elsa told him, "You need a rest, Albert. I've brought you a nice glass of warm milk and a biscuit. I will leave it on the bedside table in your room."

Einstein looked up from his desk at his caring, supportive wife, his large, sad, brown eyes communicating to her his disappointment at another night of fruitless labor. He had married his first cousin, Elsa, after a tempestuous first marriage to a fellow student in Zurich, the melancholic Mileva, who bore him two sons. While no one could say his union with Elsa was one of great passion, it was a marriage of great mutual respect, basically a platonic relationship based on friendship that gave both what they needed most: for him, a peaceful home life in which to conduct his work; for her, the mission to serve as support for a great man.

"It's very kind of you, Elsa. I will soon be off to bed. Please don't worry yourself about me. I'll not stay up very much later. I promise."

Nodding, Elsa turned and quietly closed the study door behind her, leaving Einstein to his dreams and reflections. Taking up his pipe to discard the plug of tobacco in the trash bin beneath the desk, Einstein's ruminations turned once again to the role fate had played in bringing him to Princeton.

⋮

In the winter of 1932 Einstein visited the California Institute of Technology (Caltech) in Pasadena to deliver a series of lectures. Unknown to him, less than two years earlier the Bamberger family, wealthy New Jersey department store magnates, had provided an extremely generous endowment for the establishment of an "institute for advanced study" in Princeton, New Jersey, and commissioned the educator, Abraham Flexner, to make it a reality. Flexner also happened to be in

Pasadena at the same time as Einstein and made a call on the great physicist to get his opinion on how to develop the new institute. As fate would have it, at that very time the political situation in Germany was going from bad to worse, and just a few months earlier Einstein had been the focus of a vicious attack on "Jewish physics" by sychophants of the Nazi regime whose vitriolic aim was to try to discredit scientific work done by any Jewish researchers. As a result, Einstein decided that he would have to leave Germany and was thus sensitized to opportunities abroad. Of course, there was no shortage of opportunities for the world's greatest scientist. But it had to be the *right* opportunity.

As soon as he heard about the new institute, Einstein liked the idea. So he listened quite closely to Flexner as the two of them strode back and forth across the small Caltech campus discussing various aspects of the new institute's formation. Just before the end of Flexner's short stay in California, Einstein saw him again and they agreed to meet the following spring when they would both be in Oxford.

Six months later, on a sunny day in May, Flexner and Einstein were strolling across the grounds of Christ Church College in Oxford when Flexner decided to roll the dice. He said straight out that if Einstein was interested in joining the new Institute, he was welcome under whatever terms he cared to name. Not a man to make a hasty decision, Einstein hesitated. He remembered that he had already turned down an offer from Princeton University back in 1927. But conditions had changed. Maybe it was now time to reconsider crossing the Atlantic—for good. Yet again the two men agreed to meet, this time at Einstein's summer home in Caputh, Germany, the very next month. Flexner stayed for eight hours that day, and left with Einstein's answer: "I am fire and flame for it," he told Flexner. And so it came to pass that on June 4, 1932, Einstein became the first faculty member of the fledgling Institute for

Advanced Study. Overnight, the IAS was on the worldwide intellectual map with a vengeance. Instant respectability!

How droll, Einstein chuckled to himself, that his relations with Flexner soured almost immediately. First, there was the fight to persuade Flexner to accept his assistant, Walther Mayer, on equal terms as an Institute Professor. I almost had to resign before I even took up the position in Princeton, Einstein recalled, just to show Flexner how important Mayer was to my work.

The next crisis came from Flexner's pathological need to keep the whole faculty, especially his star scientist, isolated from the real world. Einstein remembered how Flexner went so far as to intercept his letters, telegrams, even an invitation to the White House! It got so bad that at one point Einstein wrote letters to close friends in which he wrote the return address as "Concentration Camp, Princeton."

But Einstein had the last laugh—a big one. By early 1939 he had had enough of Flexner's pettiness and meddling in his affairs. And so had many of the other faculty members. So a *coup d'état* was hatched with, of all people, Einstein as the ringleader. What a glorious moment that was, thought Einstein, replaying the episode in his mind. The plot to unseat Flexner was hatched at a meeting, Einstein presiding, at the Nassau Tavern, a block from the Princeton University campus. But who would have ever expected otherwise? After all, here was one of the great rebels of all time. A man who championed the rights of individuals against repressive political regimes. A man who defied the demigods of his own profession to create and walk a path that no man had walked before. Who better to be the moving force behind the removal of the dictatorial Flexner? Ah, those were the days, he laughed, before the war cast its long shadow over most of the world.

The furrows in Einstein's leonine brow were particularly evident when he reflected on his role in encouraging

President Roosevelt to develop the atomic bomb. It pained him deeply that many people thought his famous formula $E = mc^2$, expressing the vast amount of energy contained in particulate matter, was an essential aspect of "the bomb." As a long-time pacifist and vehement supporter of the peaceful resolution of conflict, Einstein would have been the last to advocate nuclear force—if he had seen any alternative to halt the Nazi movement for world domination. But even in such an emotionally charged environment, he doubted that the letter he signed, at the instigation of his friend Leo Szilard, and sent to President Franklin D. Roosevelt, was a deciding factor in the establishment of the Manhattan Project, which would translate his formula into an actual weapon. Many other forces were at work at the time, all pushing in this same direction, and the biggest effect Einstein believed his letter could have had was to advance the timing of the project by a few weeks.

When the first bomb was dropped on Hiroshima, he thought, "Oh, horrible!" Nothing would ever convince him that this act was forgivable in either moral or military terms. But the bomb was a reality. So what should he do? What should anyone do? He campaigned long and hard for a world state. He sadly felt that in the end, the result of these untiring efforts was to make him even more distrustful of both the United States and the Soviet Union. The times in America now were just not right for such ideas, he concluded. These were times for very conservative views of the sort advocated by Johnny von Neumann, who stated that a preemptive strike on the Soviet Union was *necessary.* In von Neumann's words, "If you say such a strike would be good but not until tomorrow, I say why not today?" I am just an old sinner, Einstein thought, lost in a world of ever-shifting values and desires. I've been put out to pasture in this village of demigods on stilts just to *be* here. I'm an icon, a landmark, but not a beacon. The world of today belongs to the separatists, the militarists, the rabble rousers, and the flag-waving nationalists.

Sometimes Einstein wondered why he became so caught up in these political and moral matters. He remembered a conversation he had had a few years earlier with his then assistant, Ernst Straus. Straus also wondered about the balance of time Einstein spent between the political and the scientific. Einstein recalled saying that, "Yes, we have to divide our time like that, between our politics and our equations. But to me our equations are far more important, for politics is only a matter of present concern. A mathematical equation stands forever." Whoever finds a thought that enables us to obtain a slightly deeper glimpse into the eternal secrets of nature has been given great grace, he believed, and this far transcends the merely personal or political.

Such thoughts are dangerous, he joked to himself. They brought back visions of the intense lobbying Johnny von Neumann had been doing recently to gather support for building his computing machine. Von Neumann's discussion with him about this machine some weeks earlier at the Institute had brought him face to face with an entirely different side of the scientific enterprise than he had previously encountered. Could such a device have any use in furthering his own work on the unified field theory? What could it mean to *anyone's* work at the Institute? Do such machines represent a new wave in the practice of science, as Johnny claims? Or are they simply glorified calculators? These questions intruded so forcefully on his thoughts this night that he finally threw down his fountain pen and gave them full rein.

It is ironic that von Neumann should concern himself with what, in essence, is an experimental activity, thought Einstein, since it doesn't seem to me that Johnny has the physicist's natural feeling for, and recourse to, experiment. While he certainly knows a good deal of physics, his interest in the physical always seems to center on the mathematical formalization of a physical situation, not the physics itself. Einstein thought that such an axiomatic approach to physical theories bore the same relation to physics as grammar bore to literature. So why was Johnny so deeply concerned with a problem in engineering?

Einstein had totally missed the point of what a computer is for. In statements on the relevance of such a device for his own work, he repeatedly joked that he didn't see how a calculator would get him any closer to the chimerical unified field theory he so diligently sought. Scientific knowledge of a type could, perhaps, be teased out of Nature's grasp by performing an especially lengthy or intricate calculation. And Johnny's machine would be of great value for that. But there's more to science than doing a calculation, thought Einstein, strangely oblivious to the lengthy calculations he himself had performed by hand to develop his own general theory of relativity.

Von Neumann might have been amused by Einstein's blindness to what he saw as the obvious virtues of computing machines. Von Neumann always thought that Einstein had a certain kind of contempt for other physicists, including even the very best and most famous ones, because he had been lionized and even deified so much. After all, no one ever tried to invent something that would improve or rival or change the general theory of relativity. Von Neumann also felt that Einstein didn't think much of others as possible rivals in the physics of the twentieth century. So why should he think much of the ideas of an outsider like von Neumann about a device that he would prefer to replace with a fountain pen?

Can a machine stand in for the human mind? Can a machine think creative thoughts, creative enough to crack the puzzle of the unified field? Einstein felt that he must take up those questions with Gödel on their walk tomorrow. He leaned back in his chair, stretched his arms, and considered how Gödel might react to the idea of a machine that thinks like a man.

Einstein knew from von Neumann that two researchers at the University of Chicago, Warren McCulloch and Walter Pitts, had constructed a mathematical model of the neuronal structure making up the brain, showing that it was equivalent in its information-processing capability to a computing machine. This result caused von Neumann, along with others, to wonder whether a computing machine might one day surpass even the cognitive abilities of the human brain. Einstein scoffed at such hubris. Where is the human spirit in such a network of neurons? Where is the creative drive, the soul? It's inconceivable, he thought, that a box of metal, glass, wires, and electronic tubes could in any way duplicate the brain. Perhaps I should give my active support to von Neumann's project, just so that he can build this machine and discover this self-evident fact for himself. How can someone as smart and perceptive as Johnny be so blind as to believe that the human mind is nothing more than a machine? Kurt will have a good laugh over this when I speak to him about it tomorrow, he chuckled to himself, as he envisioned Gödel's incredulous look when faced with this astounding claim.

The thought of Gödel brought back images of the emotional stress this business of his promotion to Professor was visiting upon his friend. Einstein thought again of the unpleasantness with Flexner over the appointment of his assistant, Walther Mayer, to a full-fledged professorship at the Institute. In that instance, he was able to use his leverage on Flexner to push through the position for Mayer. Gödel's case should actually be much easier, Einstein thought, since no one disputed the brilliance of his work, quite unlike the meagre corpus he had been able to present in support of Mayer's candidacy for the faculty. But I have no influence any longer on those who will decide Gödel's fate, he ruefully acknowledged. I'm simply an icon, useful to the Institute for my name and face, but completely cut off from the mainstream of all its intellectual and professional activities.

Einstein was continually puzzled by the energy and enthusiasm that people put into trying to exert power over others, pursue material gain, and generally involve themselves in the ephemeral affairs of everyday life. In spirit, if not in intellect, he was the most Platonistic of men, believing that, while the world is definitely "out there," the life of the mind completely transcends it. The whole point of science for him was summed up in his belief, along with Schopenhauer's, that one of the strongest motives that lead men to art and science is escape from everyday life with its painful crudity and hopeless dreariness, from the fetters of one's own ever-shifting desires. A finely tempered nature longs to escape from the personal life into the world of objective perception and thought. And with this uplifting manifesto on his mind, he gathered himself up from the desk and laid down his pipe. Turning out the light, he left his study to go to bed and thought yet again, tomorrow is another day. Maybe, just maybe, it will be *the* day . . . .

Chapter Seven

AN EVENING AT OLDEN MANOR

Olden Manor, the Institute for Advanced Study's Director's rambling, two-story, white clapboard house, would be alive with physicists on this lovely spring evening, thought Oppie, as he waited on the front porch to welcome his dinner guests. The first to arrive was Wolfgang Pauli.

"Welcome, Wolfgang," said Oppie, greeting Pauli warmly with a handshake and ushering him into the entrance hall. "The first to arrive is always the luckiest. He gets first shot at the appetizers and drinks. They're on the side table in the living room. Please help yourself and I'll join you shortly."

As Pauli moved off to the living room to join Oppie's wife, Kitty, who was already finishing off a double shot of bourbon and water, Oppie returned to the front door to welcome his next guest, the young postdoctoral visitor to the university and his former student at Berkeley, David Bohm. Dressed in typical academic style in casual tweeds and a sweater, the unassuming, gentle Bohm's hazel eyes sparked with a lively intelligence. Oppie was pleased that David had come to the gathering tonight, as he was quite sure the young man would benefit enormously from the lively discussion promised by the other physicists who would be around the table. What a pity, thought Oppie, that Einstein had another engagement and could not be here tonight. But, then, perhaps it's just as well, as Bohm has much of his own to offer to tonight's gathering, and the overshadowing presence of Einstein might get in the way. Besides, thought Oppie, it will be interesting to see how the others react to Bohm's ideas, since very few people know that David is working with Einstein on, of all things, Einstein's *bête noire,* quantum theory.

Hard on Bohm's heels was the slight, cadaverous-looking Hungarian-American physicist from Princeton University, Eugene Wigner. A schoolmate of von Neumann in Budapest in his youth, Wigner was one of the four Hungarians—von Neumann, Edward Teller, and Leo Szilard being the others—who came to the United States in the 1930s and gave rise to the joke that those who claimed aliens had landed in ancient Egypt or South America were wrong; they had obviously landed in Budapest! Unlike his three compatriots, however, who were noted for their eccentricities and brusqueness, Wigner was soft-spoken, unfailingly courteous, and completely normal in every apparent way. As he shook Oppie's hand at the doorway, Wigner quietly asked in his faint Hungarian accent, "Has Bethe yet arrived?" referring to Hans Bethe, from Cornell University, in whose honor tonight's dinner was arranged. "Not yet," Oppie replied. "But I expect him any moment. Meanwhile, please come in and make yourself at home," as he waved his arm in the general direction of the living room, inviting Wigner to join the others.

As he stood alone in the entrance hall awaiting Bethe's arrival, Oppie thought back to the days at Los Alamos when Bethe headed the Manhattan Project's Theoretical Division. What a dynamo the little German was, presiding over what the Project's military leader, General Leslie R. Groves, had called "the biggest collection of eggheads ever assembled." But Bethe's drive, personality, and overpowering intellect, together with the shared sense of urgency to get the job done, was the perfect combination to harness that talented but unruly group. It will be very good indeed, thought Oppenheimer, to see Bethe again. And just as that thought began to fade, the man himself appeared at the door. Short, with a round, pugnacious face and bushy blond hair, Bethe bore a striking resemblance to the hen-pecked tycoon Jiggs, in the comic strip *Bringing Up Father*. His manner was as much like that of a longshoreman from Hamburg as of a physics professor from Cornell. But no one could deny his brilliance or his insight into the physics of the atomic nucleus, not to mention his sensitivity to the interface between science and human values, a trait finely honed by his spearheading of the theoretical work underlying development of the atomic bomb at Los Alamos.

Oppenheimer rubbed his hands in anticipation of the evening's festivities as he followed Bethe into the house. They joined the others, who were gathered in the living room around the slim, dark-haired, fiery-tempered Kitty Oppenheimer, who as always, had a drink in one hand and a cigarette in the other. Oppie gazed at his wife from afar for a moment, wondering, not for the first time, whether her unstable nature and heavy drinking would yet transform his first marriage into her fourth divorce. Well, there was nothing for it, he thought, but to join the party and do his best to divert the discussion back into more cerebral—and intellectually productive—

directions than Kitty's loud and slightly off-color story seemed to be taking it. Striding up to the group, Oppie smiled and his presence was felt by everyone. They turned to give the floor to him, not only as the Director of the IAS and the host of tonight's dinner, but also as the intellectual leader he had been to all of them.

As might have been expected, the voluble Pauli opened the cocktail discussion by enquiring of Oppenheimer, "Tell us, Robert, how are you dealing with this bunch of crackpots and geniuses here in Princeton? In Los Alamos you had a war to win; here the only war is between the physicists and the mathematicians—with you in the middle. I wonder if refereeing this battle of wills isn't even more difficult than managing the building of a bomb?"

Oppenheimer raised an eyebrow and smiled at this remark, saying slightly sarcastically, "Pauli, you never cease to amaze. Now why would you think there is any tension here at the IAS? You know we are all here to engage in deep thought of the most Platonic variety, not to backbite, gossip, maneuver, scheme, or belittle. How one might ever feel otherwise is beyond me. Perhaps another drink will help ease your mind on this count."

Bethe couldn't resist the temptation to poke a bit of fun at Oppenheimer either, as he added, "I hardly think Pauli is exaggerating the situation much, if at all, Robert. You have the mathematicians fighting among themselves over Gödel's promotion. You have the entire faculty divided over Johnny's flight of computing fancy. And now you have your own problems with the trustees, especially Admiral Strauss, and your role in national security deliberations on nuclear weapons. And these are just the most obvious matters, the things that everyone sees. Don't you sometimes wish you were back on The Hill in Los Alamos?"

Nodding vigorously, Pauli couldn't resist throwing in one

more jibe: "Yes, this Institute is really a snakepit. I wonder how much more real physics or even mathematics might be done if these geniuses focused more on their work and less on their colleagues."

Oppenheimer's penetrating blue eyes turned cold as ice as he stared daggers at Pauli, pausing momentarily to light a cigarette before replying. But before he could offer a riposte to Pauli's acerbic remarks, Kitty gaily broke in to tell the group that they were being rude to her husband and that they must all join her in a toast to the man who had brought them together tonight. To further ease the tension, Wigner softly seconded Kitty's proposal, adding in his charmingly polite and self-effacing manner, "Yes, Kitty. No one in this room deserves our respect more than Robert. He has turned the IAS into one of the world's leading centers for theoretical physics in just a couple of years. I say we focus on this achievement and leave these petty academic disputes to the academics. I raise my glass to you, Robert."

As all present held their glasses high and wished Oppie the best, a bell sounded from the next room indicating that the cook was ready to serve the meal. Kitty Oppenheimer quickly began to gather the group together like a mother hen, leading them into the dining room. They were greeted by the sight of a lovely Georgian table fully set for a formal dinner, even down to the elegant touch of handwritten place cards. Oppenheimer and his wife sat at opposite ends of the long table. As the guests found their places and settled in, Oppenheimer stood to formally welcome everyone.

"Kitty joins me in welcoming you all to Olden Manor tonight. I'm especially pleased to have my old teacher, Pauli, here, together with my own student, David Bohm. It's not often in a group of six people that one finds three generations of physicists. I'm sure that will spark some interesting discussions before the evening is over. So let me say no more other than to offer this small toast: To the overall health of theoretical physics. May the unified field theory remain forever elusive!"

A general round of laughter broke out at this last remark, which referred to Oppie's confirming the generally held belief among theoretical physicists that Einstein's decades-long quest was the physicists' version of the quest for the Holy Grail: full of hope, adventure, romance, and naïveté, but ultimately doomed to noble failure.

At each place also was a small card announcing the menu for the dinner, a rather more formal gesture than usual for a dinner at the Oppenheimers. In fact, a more typical dinner was a handful of friends sitting around the kitchen table for a couple of hours of pretty heavy drinking, followed by Kitty finally going to the stove to rustle up a pot of chili and some fried eggs. But tonight was special. Oppie really wanted to talk some physics, and had invited a stellar cast of conversational partners for the occasion. The menu reflected the event: cold gazpacho for the warm spring evening, followed by a Caesar salad, broiled filet of sole almondine, a light lemon sorbet, and finally a dessert of German chocolate cake with coffee. Nothing too exotic or gourmet, but still something special in these years immediately following the wartime shortages, and a perfect choice for the hotter than normal weather in Princeton this spring.

"Tell, us, David," said Oppenheimer addressing his former student, Bohm, "what kind of work are you doing with Einstein nowadays? Most of us think the Old Man is completely off the track in his pursuit of the unified field theory and totally out of touch with reality with his resolutely classical attitude to quantum theory."

Bohm shifted uncomfortably in his chair, startled to be called upon in this way to render judgment on the greatest physicist of the century, and to have to do it before such icons as Pauli and Wigner and Bethe, not to mention his teacher,

Oppenheimer. But Bohm was not in Princeton without reason, and he had a definite point of view on the matter of quantum theory that also departed substantially from the conventional wisdom of the Copenhagen school. So while his cocktail-party chatter was self-effacing and modest to the point of deference, when it came to expounding his views on physics he was a veritable tiger, gesticulating with abandon and asserting his unconventional views with all the vigor of a young man carving out a position for himself in the world of adults. In this mode he stated with conviction, "I think Einstein's position on quantum theory has been seriously misunderstood by many physicists. They seem to think that he believes the theory is completely wrong-headed and longs for a return to the classical view of Newton. In one sense that is correct: Einstein *does* long for part of that classical view."

"And which part is that?" interrupted Wigner, setting down his glass and looking intently at Bohm. "I suppose I must be one of those many physicists who think he rejects the theory entirely. This is certainly one case in which I'd like to be wrong."

"The part of classical physics Einstein clings to tenaciously," answered Bohm, "is that objects—quantum or otherwise—have well-defined properties like position and momentum and energy *at all times.* He steadfastly holds to this view, and is totally unsympathetic to the idea that such properties mysteriously come into existence only when an object is observed, and that before a measurement the object has only a probability of being in a certain position or having a particular momentum."

Pauli had been squirming in his chair since Bohm had uttered his first word and could no longer contain himself. "Yes, yes, I think we have all heard Einstein state this view at one time or another. Even my Austrian colleague, Schrödinger, who created the wave function that we all now, after Max

Born's suggestion, interpret as characterizing this probability, felt uncomfortable with this interpretation. But you cannot change the facts. And it is a fact that the predictions of this statistical interpretation have never yet failed to be confirmed by every experiment that's been done to check them."

"Yes," chimed in Bethe enthusiastically. "Can a scientific theory be wrong if it agrees with every experimental test we can devise to check it?"

"Well, the history of science is filled with examples of theories that agreed with experiments and predicted new observations very well, yet were later shown to be wrong," Oppenheimer retorted. "What about the Ptolemaic theory that described planetary motion as a sequence of cycles piled upon cycles piled upon cycles? The weight of all those cycles eventually sank the theory; it just wasn't simple enough to satisfy our aesthetic sense, although it certainly gave accurate predictions of where the planets would be found."

"Precisely," said Pauli, asserting that "there is more to a theory than just being right. There is an aesthetic dimension. And that's what seems to be at the heart of Einstein's objection to our current view of quantum theory. It is not aesthetic enough for his taste. The laws of nature must be not only understandable, but also beautiful. And the rules we use in quantum mechanics to make predictions about material objects defy 'reasonable' interpretation. They just don't satisfy his standard for how things ought to be. Or at least that seems to be Einstein's view."

Oppenheimer waved his fork in Bohm's direction, almost dropping a tasty-looking tidbit of anchovy from the Caesar salad in the process. The gesture silenced the table, as all wondered about the fate of the anchovy. Would it fall or not? When it did not, Oppie gave the floor back to Bohm who continued: "There's no doubt that the standard Copenhagen interpretation accounts for everything that we have ever observed. But the idea that objects with well-defined properties don't *really* exist unless they are being observed seems preposterous—and not just to Einstein. I also find it aesthetically very unsatisfactory. So my conversations with Einstein mostly center on exploring a viable alternative interpretation."

Oppenheimer, of course, knew Bohm was not just speculating but had actually developed just such an interpretation, or at least the idea for one. Always the teacher, he prodded his reticent student into telling the group what he thought might be a better way to view the quantum situation. Bohm looked rather like a deer caught in a bright spotlight as all eyes turned to him. As a mere postdoc amidst this star-studded cast, he was extremely hesitant to present his "heretical" ideas. But he also knew he'd never have a better opportunity to get the thoughts of the world's greatest quantum theorists about those ideas. This was enough to overcome his nervous fears.

"My view is really a revival of an idea floated by Prince Louis de Broglie a decade or so ago. Basically, it involves regarding an object like an electron as being a classical particle *at all times.* So it has definite properties like position at all times, too. But associated with every such object is a wave of information I call the *quantum potential.*"

"Is this a real wave?" asked Bethe, "or is it a kind of mathematical wave like the wave function described by Schrödinger's equation?"

"No, it is a real wave," Bohm hastened to explain. "Its role is in some sense to probe the environment and transmit this information back to its associated particle. The particle then behaves in a manner consistent with the information it receives about the environment from the quantum potential."

As Bohm noted at the outset, this idea of the *pilot wave* was not new. The French quantum theorist de Broglie had advanced the notion in the 1920s. But he ran into almost insurmountable mathematical obstacles in making it work, and so it was more or less laughed out of court by proponents of the then dominant paradigm coming from Copenhagen; that is, from Danish physicist Niels Bohr and coworkers. However, Bohm thought he had figured out how to get around the mathematical problems. But the group immediately focused on other, far more evident, problems with the whole scheme. Pauli got things going by asking, "You say this quantum potential is a real wave. So why hasn't anyone ever detected it? If it's real, then we should be able to measure it, don't you think?"

"I agree," chimed in Bethe. "If you can't measure it, at least in principle, then it doesn't exist. It's just a mathematical construct added to make things more complicated, not simpler."

Oppenheimer had to jump in to defend Bohm. "Just a minute," he said quickly. "I think recovery of an objective, classical reality is worth a lot. Maybe it's worth enough even to swallow an unobservable pilot wave of the sort David is suggesting. After all, how many of us have seen or even measured a positron? Yet we have no trouble at all believing they exist. Initially, they came out of Dirac's formulation of quantum theory to fill a mathematical gap in his setup; later, Carl Anderson discovered how to measure them. Bohm's wave might follow the same path."

Wigner quietly tapped the side of his glass to get the group's attention. Everyone knew that when he spoke, whatever he had to say would be well thought out and not an off-the-cuff shot from the lip. So they all turned to hear the clever Hungarian's thoughts on Bohm's idea.

"I'm not especially worried about the measurability of this pilot wave. But it would be ironic in the extreme if Einstein endorsed this way of restoring classical properties to quantum objects since, as this young man describes things, the quantum potential seems to violate Einstein's own special theory of relativity."

"What do you mean?" asked Oppie incredulously, staring at Wigner.

"Well, as I understand it, this quantum potential has to probe the environment in some way and then communicate this information back to the particle. This communication must be faster than light, for the particle to adjust its behavior to accommodate whatever attribute—position, momentum, spin—the measuring device has been set up to measure. But this kind of superluminal signaling is exactly what Einstein's own theory forbids."

The table fell silent. As always, the thoughtful Wigner had hit exactly upon the weakest link in Bohm's entire setup. It would seem that either the special theory of relativity or Bohm's theory would have to go. No one cared to place any bets on the survival of the pilot wave theory if it came down to *that*. But Bohm's intellect was made of sterner stuff, and he had a ready answer to Wigner's objection.

"To be more precise," Bohm stated calmly, "Einstein's theory says that no *material* object can transcend the speed of light. But he says nothing about immaterial objects. The quantum potential is a wave of active information, not a wave of matter. So it can have effects at long distances and does not dissipate like a sound or water wave. So I do not believe this superluminal objection applies, at all."

Pauli was not finished with this story, though. Jutting out his chin pugnaciously, he asked, "So you think the superluminal effect can be seen only when we look at the correlations between signals at two separated locations. But if we look at what's happening in the immediate neighborhood of either location, there is no superluminal effect. Right?"

"Precisely," Bohm replied at an almost superluminal speed himself. "I think relativity is a statistical effect, not an absolute one. And the statistical properties of signals are totally independent when we look in the local neighborhood of one location or the other. They show up only when the locations are separated."

"Well, David, this is certainly an intriguing idea," said Oppenheimer approvingly. I think we'll have to schedule you very soon to present these ideas in more formal clothing at our weekly physics seminar. But now I see the cook signaling that it's time for the fish. So let's let David quickly finish up his salad before all the plates disappear."

⋮

Leaning back in his chair to allow the servant to remove his salad plate, Oppie's mind took a break from the complex and demanding conundrums of theoretical physics, as he remembered his own path from a privileged, precocious childhood in Manhattan to the directorship of the IAS. After finishing a bachelor's degree at Harvard in 1925 after just three years of study, he traveled in Europe for several years, doing research in Cambridge and then Göttingen, where he received his doctorate in 1927. It was in Germany that he wrote a famous paper with his doctoral advisor, Max Born, on the quantum theory of molecules that formed the basis for quantum studies of molecules after that time. Upon his return to the United States, Oppie found himself in the unusual situation of having two halftime positions, spending the fall and winter at the University of California at Berkeley, the spring at Caltech. As an indication of his students' love for him and his influence on his students, many of them made the same migration each fall and spring to remain continuously under his tutelage.

As the filet of sole was served, Oppenheimer thought back fondly to the period in Berkeley when he was building his school of theoretical physics. Students like Bohm were drawn to his mesmerizing lecturing style and general scientific attitude, which shaped their own work and lives thereafter. But the drums of war were beginning to beat louder, and he was eager to serve the American war effort. He got his chance in 1942, when he was appointed leader of the theoretical effort to design the atomic bomb.

"Robert!" came the shrill voice of Kitty, breaking into Oppenheimer's reverie, catapulting him back to the present. "Why don't you fill everyone's wine glass and stop daydreaming about your past successes?"

Dutiful host that he was, Oppie poured white wine all around, as Hans Bethe tried to make light of Kitty's aggressive tone by remarking sympathetically, "Well, Robert certainly has a lot to reminisce about. Thinking of those days in Los Alamos, I'd venture. And why not? It's hard to believe that they were only a couple of years ago. So much has happened since. But what a time! And what a collection of people and problems. I'd daydream too, if I were you, Robert."

"I don't think it was all that wonderful," carped Kitty, not to be mollified so easily by Bethe's attempt to gracefully turn the conversation. "It was boring being on top of that mountain with all those physicists," she continued, seemingly unaware that at that moment she was surrounded by many members of that very group. "And the security and military guards made it even more horrid than being surrounded by the eggheads here in Princeton."

As Kitty momentarily interrupted her tirade to take a long pull from her wine glass, the ever-polite and charming Wigner immediately stepped in to do some damage control and bring a measure of civility back to the table.

"The entire Manhattan Project—not just the part in Los Alamos, for which the entire nation must thank Robert—but also the gaseous production of plutonium in Hanford and Oak Ridge, Fermi's atomic pile in Chicago, and all the other facilities involved will be remembered as the beginning of the marriage between science and government. This may well turn out to be a Faustian bargain, but I don't believe we scientists can walk away from it now. The best we can do is make every effort to exert whatever influence we have to bring about the most peaceful and constructive uses of our efforts. Don't you agree, Robert?"

Here was a theme dear to Oppenheimer's heart—and Bethe's, too: the social responsibility of the scientist. "How do you view this dilemma, Hans?" asked Oppie with real curiosity. "After all, you led the theoretical effort at Los Alamos. Do you think the individual scientist is responsible for his actions?"

"My position on that has always been clear," replied Bethe firmly. "I believe that each scientist is indeed responsible for his own individual actions. But scientists *collectively* have no right to refuse work on weapons of mass destruction if the cause is just. And I firmly believe that our cause in Los Alamos was as just as any cause can be."

"And how do you feel, now that the war is over, about how these weapons should be controlled?" asked Bohm. "Should they be handed over to the military just like any other weapon? Or do they represent such a major jump in destructive power over all previous weapons that they must be handled differently?"

"There is no doubt in my mind," interrupted Wigner, "that these weapons should be under the control of a civilian authority. They are not merely weapons; their use has such symbolic significance that it cannot be left to narrow military concerns."

"So use of the atomic bomb is a political act. Is that what you are saying?" said Pauli, finally joining the discussion.

Before the reticent Wigner could formulate a reply, Oppenheimer asserted his view of how atomic weapons should be handled. "I believe firmly that we need an international authority to control all atomic energy work, on weapons or otherwise. Such an agency should develop atomic reactors for power and other peaceful uses, not simply serve as a policeman to prevent individual nations from developing atomic energy and weapons on their own. So, yes, *anything* to do with atomic energy, not just the use of atomic bombs, is political."

"Do you really think such a plan is workable?" asked Bethe.

"To be truthful, no. I think the only organization that could provide the basis for it is the United Nations, and it's my belief that any plan of this sort will be immediately vetoed by the Russians. If indeed this comes to pass, the United States will have little choice but to develop reliable methods for detecting foreign nuclear weapons tests so we can keep abreast of nuclear weapons development in Russia and everywhere else in the world."

"As Chairman of the Atomic Energy Commission's Nuclear Advisory Committee you should be well positioned to exert influence to make that happen," Bethe noted approvingly.

"Yes," added Wigner in a somewhat gloomy tone, shaking his head as he did so. "It does appear as if this will be the way things will work out. It's a sad business for mankind. Atomic energy can be used to help so many people. Yet the money and brainpower will almost entirely be channeled into making destructive weapons of even greater power."

Bethe followed this unhappy lament with the surprisingly casual remark, "If what I hear from Los Alamos is true, things are only going to become worse, not better."

At the offhand nature of this comment, Bohm's head shot up, and with some intensity in his voice he asked Bethe, "What do you mean 'worse'? How can things be worse than they are right now? For the first time in history we have a weapon that can literally destroy the human race. What could be worse than that?"

"Ah, therein lies a tale that may well define human relations for this century—and before it's even half over," Oppie answered for Bethe. "Let me tell you that story, David."

Oppenheimer went on to tell Bohm and the others about ongoing debates in Washington, sparked off by a proposal from Berkeley physicist Edward Teller, to build an even grander nuclear weapon nicknamed the "Super." Teller, another Hungarian emigré of the same generation and hawkish political leanings as von Neumann, believed strongly that the Soviets would do everything in their power to match—and possibly surpass—American hegemony in atomic weaponry. As a result, he lobbied vociferously in both the scientific and political communities to build a bomb based on nuclear *fusion* rather than fission. This was the process that went on in the heart of the sun to transform hydrogen into helium, and Teller believed that by employing a conventional atomic bomb to squeeze the hydrogen together, the very same process could be duplicated in a nuclear weapon with vastly greater destructive power than was possible with the bomb activated by the fission process. This was because the energy involved in forcing like-charged nuclear particles such as two protons to "fuse" when they want to stay apart is vastly greater than the energy released when a large atomic nucleus like uranium-235 throws off neutrons; that is, "splits" in a fission process. The trick is how to force the nuclear particles to stay together long enough to get the fusion process going.

"But," said Oppie, continuing his story, "there are a number of scientists and politicians, myself among them, who think Teller's proposal is both technically questionable and morally indefensible."

Pauli, who strongly supported Oppenheimer's position, quickly added, "I think as you do, Robert, that the United States should not deliberately start an arms race, and should first at least make some effort to speak with the Russians about coming to an agreement not to develop these hydrogen weapons. Besides, as far as I know, there is no technical basis for thinking that such a weapon could be constructed even if the government were to give the effort its blessing."

"For the sake of argument, I think it should be noted that there was no guarantee that the atomic bomb could actually be built either," interjected Wigner. "It's one thing to create a sustained fission reaction in a laboratory; it's quite something else to recreate that process in a weapon that's small enough to be delivered to its target by an airplane. Yet it was accomplished."

After everyone had his say, Oppenheimer turned to Bethe and asked what he thought about Teller's proposal. "After all, Hans," he said, leaning forward and putting his arms on the table, "you have more hands-on experience at weapons design than anyone at the table. Do you believe the Super should be built?"

Bethe squirmed uncomfortably in his chair as he considered Oppie's question. Finally, he scooted his chair forward, put his elbows on the table, and looked Oppenheimer in the eye as he said, "Personally, I would not want to work on such a device—even if it were shown to be technically doable. I said earlier that I strongly believe that each individual scientist is responsible for his own actions. I must say that I had similar misgivings about working on the Manhattan Project, but upon reflection, each step, taken on its own, seemed so logical that I finally agreed. Sometimes I wish I were a more consistent idealist."

Oppenheimer seemed to be tiring of this line of conversation and was ready to direct discussion into other channels when Bethe added, "You know, Robert, I think you are running a grave risk with your vocal opposition to Teller's proposal, especially in the corridors of power in Washington. Teller has many friends in high places and to have you, the 'father' of the atomic bomb, come out so strongly against his proposal could spell a lot of trouble for you."

"It already has. You probably know that Admiral Strauss has been lobbying for my removal as director of the IAS. I suppose my youthful fling with the Communist Party, not to mention my brother Frank's even more active role in Communist affairs here, doesn't do me any good, either," murmured Oppenheimer. "But this business of escalation of an arms race is much more important than any individual. I simply must speak out against it."

Kitty, of all people, jumped in to rescue her husband from this dreary, depressing discussion, as she cried out loudly, "Time to refill the glasses. Now let's talk about something a bit more cheery, like what else physics has to say about the real world besides bigger and better weapons."

As the cook brought out dishes of lemon sorbet, Bohm recalled the conversation on the limits to scientific knowledge in which he had participated at von Neumann's party a week or so earlier. He remembered the conversation centering on the strictly logical limits of science—how much could one really *know* about the real world by employing the methods and techniques of science? But here, he thought, is a very different sort of "limits" question: How much *should* scientists try to know about the workings of nature? This was a moral issue, one involving scientists' consciences more than their intellects, together with the role science should play in a free and open society. As the matter was already in the air around the table tonight, he felt no hesitation in raising it again in the context of that previous discussion at von Neumann's—but now in the reverse direction.

"We've just been considering how far scientists really should be allowed to go in their quest for understanding the inner workings of nature. This is a moral issue on the limits of the scientific enterprise. The other night at von Neumann's there was a discussion about the logical limits to science; basically, the question of what can be known about the world around us by following the scientific method. Von Neumann argued that the answer to this question is tantamount to asking about the limits to our ability to carry out a computation. As none of you was present at that discussion, I wonder what you all think about this kind of limit?"

The group sat silent for a few moments digesting this shift in the direction of the conversation. It seemed that everyone had a clear vision about the moral issue that had just been considered, if not necessarily the same vision. But this matter of logical limits was an entirely different matter and necessitated a bit of mental reorientation to consider. Pauli finally broke the silence.

"I don't believe in any such limit. There will always be things that we do not know. But that doesn't mean there is some intrinsic limitation placed upon our *ability* to know them. We didn't know about atoms at one time; now we do. We didn't know about planetary motion; now we do. Right now we don't know whether the universe will ever stop expanding and start contracting; someday we will. So I don't put a single bit of credence in the idea of this type of limit."

Bethe quickly seconded Pauli's anti-limits manifesto, adding, "I don't understand what you meant by von Neumann's remark that the limit of our science is the same as the limit of our computational capability. What can that possibly mean?"

Bohm tried to summarize von Neumann's argument from the party.

"If I have it right, von Neumann's belief is that the scientific answer to any question is the end result of following a set of rules, a kind of algorithm. For example, if you want to know about the position of an electron, you calculate the Schrödinger wave function for the experimental situation—

which is following a rule—and, if you believe the Copenhagen view of things, the result of following this rule is the probability of finding the electron at a particular location. This is the scientific answer to the question, 'Where is the electron?' "

"So, von Neumann says that following a rule is the same thing as carrying out a computation. Is that the gist of it?" asked Pauli, his eyebrows rising in some measure of skepticism.

"As I understand it, yes," confirmed Bohm.

"But what does all this business about computation have to do with nature?" wondered Wigner. "It is nice to know that the computer understands the problem. But I would like to understand it, too. And even though we put great faith in our theories, they are mathematical constructions, as is a computation, not the real world of matter and energy. Where do these fit into the overall issue of limits?"

Oppenheimer now weighed in.

"Yes, there is the nub of the matter. Our theories—and computations—are mathematical objects residing in some world outside of space and time. As such they have no clear-cut connection to real-world objects like knives, forks, tables, and chairs. Yet suitable combinations of these mathematical symbols have an uncanny way of representing real-world relationships, as with the Schrödinger equation that David just mentioned. When it comes to limits I wonder if we are talking about limits to the amount of information we can extract from the mathematical formulations. Or are we speaking about limits of our ability to probe the depths of nature? These are two entirely different questions."

As someone who had spent considerable time pondering the relationship between mathematics and physics, Wigner was highly sensitized to the ambiguity Oppenheimer had pinpointed. But just as he was about to speak to it, Pauli broke in to say, "As physicists we must be concerned with what can be known by the methods of science, not those of mathematics. Even though Galileo told us that the secrets of nature are written in the language of mathematics, in the end it is observation and experiment that tell us how nature truly is, not mathematical equations, however beautiful."

Wigner now could no longer remain silent and was literally squirming in his chair waiting for a chance to speak. After listening impatiently to Pauli's interjection, he seized his chance to declare, "I think we can all agree that the appropriateness of the language of mathematics for the formulation of the laws of physics is a wonderful gift which we neither understand nor deserve. Mathematics is simply unreasonably effective in characterizing the regularities we observe in nature. So perhaps there is a correlation between limits to what we can know in mathematics and what we can know in the physical world, too."

"This point of view brings us around to Gödel's results on the limitations of mathematical argumentation," Oppenheimer reminded the group. Gödel's results show that in any consistent logical system with sufficient expressive power to talk about ordinary arithmetic—and expressive power of such a level is certainly needed to speak about the physical world—there must be statements that can be neither proved nor disproved. Following this line of argument, we must then ask if such a statement has a correlate with some real-world phenomenon, and even more generally, what is the relationship between proving a proposition in a mathematical model and the *meaning* of that proposition in the real-world situation the model claims to represent?"

"Now we're coming the heart of the matter," declared Pauli, ever the theorist. So much a theorist, in fact, that it was rumored for years that whenever Pauli got close to a laboratory, equipment broke down, test tubes mysteriously shattered, and all sorts of other unexplainable failures started to take place. This was jokingly termed, the "Pauli Effect" by physicists worldwide.

"Yes," agreed Bohm. "This matter of logical limits immediately raises the question of the relationship between mathematical models of reality and reality itself—the map and territory, so to speak."

Wigner sharpened the question by noting that either you use a mathematical model to probe reality, in which case you have to establish the congruence between the mathematical symbols and observables in the real-world situation, or you abandon the mathematics altogether and simply correlate observations into some kind of empirical relationship expressing the regularities in the world. In the first case, you must come to terms with the fidelity of the model and perhaps Gödel-type results limiting what the mathematics can say. In the second case, the problem is how to replace the notion of mathematical proof with a concept that expresses real-world truth.

The group agreed that either horn of this dilemma is an extremely difficult and important problem in the philosophy of knowledge. Someone then brought the discussion back to the current Institute problems surrounding both von Neumann and Gödel.

"This must be an especially trying time for you, Robert," said Bethe, "having to deal at the same time with the complicated matter of Johnny's proposal to build a computer and Gödel's unhappiness at not being a Professor."

"Do you think Johnny will leave us and go elsewhere if the board doesn't approve his project? What do you think, Wigner? You've known Johnny all your life," enquired Pauli.

Speaking slowly and carefully on this point, which veered uncomfortably close to his special personal relationship with von Neumann, Wigner declared, "I know Johnny has a strong bond with the Institute and could not easily be persuaded to leave Princeton. But he is also extremely persistent when he focuses on a problem. And this computer project has captured his attention like no other problem I've ever seen him attack. So, yes, I believe that he probably will leave if the project cannot be done here. With great reluctance. But leave he will to follow this particular Muse."

Oppenheimer listened attentively to Wigner's statement, as it gave invaluable insight into how strongly von Neumann felt about the computer project. The one thing he didn't need right now was another problem with the mathematicians, who were already deeply unhappy over what they saw as him "stacking" the Institute with physicists. He would simply have to use every possible means to persuade the trustees to approve von Neumann's proposal, and let the chips fall where they might with those faculty who were against it.

"What about the situation with Gödel?" wondered Bethe. "Is the faculty in the School of Mathematics still against promoting him to Professor?"

"I'm not entirely sure how things stand on this at the moment," Oppenheimer said. "But I don't think this is as important as the von Neumann computer project problem. Gödel is not going anywhere, regardless of whether he's a Professor or a permanent Member of the Institute. This question is more a matter of his ego and the principle that intellectual work of the highest quality should be recognized by one's status in the pecking order of an organization like the IAS."

"But what else is there to fight for in the academic world except ego and position in the pecking order?" asked Pauli with a wry smile. "We certainly didn't take up the intellectual life for fame or fortune. I don't think you can dismiss Gödel's or any other academic's ego in such a cavalier fashion."

A bit stunned by Pauli's trenchant observation, Oppenheimer moved to settle things down by adding, "I did not mean to suggest that Gödel does not deserve serious consideration, only that whether he is Professor is unlikely to change the way things are done here at the IAS. Von Neumann's project is of an entirely different nature. That's all I meant."

Remembering the cocktail-party debate on limits to knowledge at von Neumann's, Bohm felt that these two problems had perhaps more in common than Oppie might want to acknowledge. "When we spoke earlier about limits to scientific knowledge, we drew the distinction between a mathematical model of a real-world situation and the situation itself. It's clear that Gödel's results on incompleteness have direct bearing on the mathematical side of this matter, as does von Neumann's claim that what we can know really comes down to what we can compute. So I think the two problems of Gödel's promotion and von Neumann's computer are not so separate as one might think."

"Well, perhaps," agreed Oppie. "The computer connection is clear. But what does this have to do with whether Gödel is a Professor or not?"

"On the surface, not much. But I think it matters for the image of the IAS as a bastion of pure thought, a home for intellectual undertakings at the boundaries of our knowledge. Making Gödel a full Professor sends a message saying the IAS acknowledges the importance of his work, not just its mathematics, but also its philosophical implications. And part of those implications relate to von Neumann's claim about what it is that science can tell us about the world."

"But only if you accept the notion that what science can tell us comes from mathematical models of the world," declared Wigner. "And we have already noted that maybe you can learn about the world without using any mathematics or computing at all."

Bethe then added: "In that case, Gödel's work is irrelevant for the limits-to-science question, wouldn't you say?"

Sensing that the conversation might be leading back into the same circle they had already gone around, Oppenheimer transparently looked at his watch, a gesture not lost on the guests, nor on his wife. Kitty stood up declaring, "I don't know about the rest of you, but I've had just about enough of Gödel, von Neumann, computers, and philosophy for one evening. I hope you'll all excuse me if I leave you to sort these deep-thought matters out among yourselves. Thank you all for coming."

Everyone took Kitty's departure as the sign that his own would not go amiss, and began offering thanks to Oppie for the evening and moving toward the entrance hall. Oppie himself breathed an inward sigh of relief at their impending departure, knowing he had a big day ahead and glad of the opportunity to get a bit of rest. Pauli spoke for all of them as he shook Oppenheimer's hand.

"Robert, it has been a great pleasure. I thank you and Kitty for the delicious dinner and stimulating conversation." Turning to the others standing with him at the doorway, he expressed his pleasure at meeting them. After a bout of hand-shaking all around, the group departed en masse and Oppenheimer was left to ponder the evening briefly before turning out the lights and walking slowly upstairs to join Kitty.

Chapter Eight

THE VERDICTS

The remnants of yesterday afternoon's talk on topological group theory were still evident in the half-erased scribblings on the blackboard in the School of Mathematics seminar room as the faculty filed in for their monthly meeting. At the small, plain, wooden table in the front of the room sat Oswald Veblen, who would chair the gathering. Veblen was the first professor hired by the Institute, and felt rightly that he was the founder of the School of Mathematics. As a result, no one ever questioned his right to chair these gatherings, a role Veblen felt might be crucial with today's agenda. Arrayed in the first couple of rows of seats facing him were the rest of the faculty: von Neumann, Morse, Siegel, and Montgomery. As Veblen scanned the faces before him to see if anyone was absent, the door opened and Hermann Weyl strode in, looking dapper, composed, and as confident in his step and manner as the most Germanic of German professors. Weyl slipped into a seat in the front row as Veblen called the meeting to order.

"Gentlemen. You all know we are here for two matters today," he declared in a voice that immediately took control of the room. "One is to consider the promotion of our colleague, Kurt Gödel, to full Professor at the Institute. The other is to choose Visiting Members for the coming academic year. As I suspect that the first agenda item will be the more time consuming of the two, I suggest we begin with consideration of Gödel's promotion. We can then deal with the visitors. Are there any objections?" Veblen asked, the look on his face saying there had better not be. "Fine. Then the floor is open for discussion of Gödel's promotion."

As soon as the words were out of Veblen's mouth, von Neumann began presenting his case in support of Gödel.

"We are all mathematicians here and so I do not think I have to acquaint anyone with the content of Gödel's work. The consensus among the world's logicians is that Gödel is by far the greatest logician of our century. Some even say he is the greatest logician since Aristotle. If our faculty had a geometer who was seriously considered in the same breath as, say, Archimedes, or a number theorist who was termed the greatest number theorist since Gauss, is there any question whether that person would be a Professor on this faculty? Gentlemen, I say again: How can any of us call ourselves 'Professor' if Gödel cannot?" Following this manifesto, von Neumann quickly took his seat, folded his hands on top of his ample paunch, and looked at the group as if to challenge any of them to dispute the airtight logic of his argument.

A few heads did nod their accord with von Neumann's impassioned plea, a rather uncommon show of emotion for the generally even-tempered Hungarian. But not everyone was in agreement. As von Neumann sat down, Weyl, as suave and full of continental style and grace as von Neumann himself, rose to address the faculty.

"There is no one here who admires Kurt as a person and as a mathematician more than I do. But as the person here closest professionally to his work—other than Johnny, of course—I feel compelled to mention that there are those who do not share Johnny's admiration for the incompleteness results that Kurt's reputation rests upon."

Von Neumann immediately jumped up and asked Weyl for details supporting this argument.

"Johnny, I'm sure you know of the Oxford philosopher, J.L. Austin."

"Indeed, I do," replied von Neumann, who in fact had never heard of Austin or a lot of other philosophers, whose work he regarded with grave suspicion and as almost totally irrelevant to the pursuit of either mathematics or the natural sciences.

"Well," continued Weyl. "When informed of Gödel's incompleteness result that says essentially that truth is always bigger than proof, Austin replied, 'Who would have ever thought otherwise?' I think this sums up the feelings of some mathematicians, too, in the sense that they feel this result is more of a trick of language than a hard result in mathematics."

"I'm sorry to have to mention," said Veblen in a rather assertive tone that made it clear he was not at all sorry to intervene, "that Hilbert himself, whom I'm sure everyone in the room will accept as a bona fide mathematician of the first rank, believed that mathematics was complete and was rather devastated when *he* was told of Gödel's achievement. So whomever these mathematicians are who minimize Gödel's accomplishment, Hilbert would not have counted himself among them. Moreover, my recollection, Hermann, is that you, yourself, have stated that Hilbert was the single greatest influence on your own development as a mathematician."

This remark coming from Veblen really took the wind out of Weyl's sails and he slowly sank back down into his chair, much like a balloon from which the air was gradually leaking. But as one sat down another jumped up, this time the ever irascible and stubborn group theorist, Deane Montgomery.

"What worries me about having Gödel as a Professor is not the merit of his mathematical work. I'm happy to accept that as being of world-class quality—stunning, in fact. It's his personality that concerns me. We have a very small faculty here, and we all know how much administrative work has to be done by each of us to manage the School of Mathematics. Even today we have to discuss and settle on applicants to be invited as visitors for the coming year. And that is but a small part of the administrative burden we each must bear. I truly wonder whether Gödel's penchant for logical precision might interfere with the smooth running of the School by introducing interminable delays while he sorts out the logical merits of the various candidates and other issues that must be decided."

Montgomery's concern reflected that of several of the faculty, since even among the extreme opinions at the IAS, Gödel's worldview and actions were very strange to a point beyond mere eccentricity. In fact, there were those who mumbled words like "certifiably insane," "crazy," and "out of touch with reality" in hushed corridor conversations about his ways. If he were made a Professor, he would acquire the responsibility, as well as the right, to become part of the decision-making process in the School of Mathematics. Some, like Montgomery, felt that the overall interests of the School were better served by leaving Gödel in his current position as a Permanent Member of the Institute, where he was not involved in administrative issues, than by elevating him to Professor, where his psychological instabilities might prove a major barrier to the School's smooth functioning.

Von Neumann and Veblen started to speak at the same time, each wanting to defuse this commonly held view of Gödel's temperament, which they both felt was an exaggerated caricature of the man's true nature. Von Neumann, especially, knew that while Gödel, like all logicians, was extremely pedantic and precise about work, he was certainly not any more other-worldly than the rest of the faculty when it came to making decisions. In fact, von Neumann felt that Gödel might inject a much-needed note of objectivity into some of the emotionally charged faculty debates on potential visitors, who were often appointed more because some faculty member wanted them as slavish collaborators than because they were the most qualified among the pool of applicants.

"Gentlemen," began von Neumann, "I have known Kurt Gödel since he was a student in Vienna in the 1920s, and so I feel I can speak with some confidence to his mindset and especially to the point that Montgomery just raised about him being a possible barrier to the administrative procedures needed to keep the School of Mathematics functioning. Gödel is a deliberative man; no doubt about that. But he most certainly is not 'crazy.' Nor is his habit of examining every logical aspect of a situation necessarily a bad thing for our faculty. For myself, I would welcome Gödel's highly logical opinion on a number of issues that we must regularly consider, including the appointment of Professors and the choice of visitors."

At this juncture Marston Morse added his voice to the discussion. He had been uncharacteristically silent, so his views carried more weight than they might have otherwise. Given his earlier antipathy to the promotion, he surprised many by giving a strong endorsement of Gödel's candidacy for Professor, standing and speaking with passion: "While I have no professional overlap with Gödel, every now and then our paths cross here at the Institute and I have raised one or another question with him about aspects of my own work. On these occasions we have even touched briefly on matters outside mathematics, including affairs of the Institute and the faculty. I have found Gödel's opinions very well thought out and at times I can hardly even begin a chain of logical argument about something without getting the impression that he has already explored that idea to all of its possible logical conclusions even before I've finished my explanation of the problem. So I agree with Johnny: Gödel will be very conscientious and thorough in carrying out his administrative duties as a Professor. I should be honored to serve on the faculty with him, and urge this body to recognize his contributions to mathematics and to the Institute by finally appointing him to the rank he so richly deserves."

Veblen, always the savvy political opportunist, saw Morse's unexpected endorsement as just the opening he needed to provide the impetus to move Gödel's promotion forward—now! Exercising his prerogative as chairman, he immediately terminated discussion and called for a vote. "We've all now had our say about Gödel. My sense of the situation is that this is the right moment to vote on the question. So unless there are any objections, I'd like each of you to write either 'Yes' or 'No' on a piece of paper and pass it up to me. 'Yes' indicates you are in favor of promoting Gödel to Professor, while 'No' means you are against it."

As Veblen passed out the pieces of paper from his notepad, there was a bit of shuffling about because the men had been caught unawares by his speedy maneuver and had to hurriedly dig in their pockets for a fountain pen or pencil to mark their ballots. An outside observer would have been amused to see the contortions some of them went through to ensure no one could see their ballots, Siegel even hunching over his chair so that he looked like he had collapsed on the spot. Eventually the papers were passed up to Veblen who gathered them together and began opening them and tallying the result.

Completing the count, which didn't take long for such a small group, Veblen turned to the group with a deadpan and said, "Gentlemen. I'm pleased to announce that we have a new Professor on our faculty today. I will inform Director Oppenheimer that the faculty of the School of Mathematics has voted in favor of promoting Kurt Gödel to Professor. Johnny, will you please communicate this result to Kurt informally? But caution him that the promotion will not be official until it is approved by the Board of Trustees."

With that simple statement, Veblen consulted his notes and suggested that the faculty move on to the next item on the agenda. And so it was that Gödel was elevated to the rank of Professor in a debate that was far more peaceful and tranquil than even his staunchest supporter, von Neumann, had expected.

⋮

Things were definitely not peaceful or tranquil in the boardroom across the hall from the mathematics seminar room. The tension between Oppenheimer and Strauss had degenerated into a kind of covert guerrilla warfare, with the two men constantly at each other's throats over Strauss's belief that Oppenheimer was a threat to national security on account of his left-leaning political and social views, as well as his prewar membership in various Communist front organizations. The animosity between them was a long-standing affair that had now boiled over. Recent rumblings from Washington suggested that Russian work on an atomic bomb had been dramatically accelerated as a result of secrets stolen from Los Alamos during Oppenheimer's reign as head of the Manhattan Project. At the moment, the two men simply glowered at each other across the boardroom table, temporarily setting aside their differences to enter into the trustees' debate on whether to overrule the faculty and confirm their earlier tentative approval of von Neumann's proposal to build a computer. Looking up from his notes while avoiding eye contact with Strauss, Oppenheimer put the matter before the board.

"At our last meeting we discussed in detail Johnny's proposal to build a computing machine here at the Institute," he stated matter-of-factly. "Since then, Johnny has told me that he is committed to this project, even to the extent of being ready to leave Princeton and go elsewhere if necessary to carry on the project. I have it on good authority that this is no idle threat, either, as he has discussed the possibility with people at several other institutions, including the University of Chicago and the Massachusetts Institute of Technology. As the faculty is strongly divided on the matter, it is really up to us here in this room to settle it. And we must do it today, as Johnny feels that there is no more time to be wasted. He wants to move forward with this project, preferably here at the IAS but elsewhere if need be."

The one thing that Oppenheimer and Strauss could agree upon was the importance of having von Neumann on the Institute faculty. They both knew that Johnny's presence in Princeton lent the Institute an air of intellectual respectability in the world of mathematics that would be difficult to replace. Moreover, as a man of the world concerned with the position of the United States in the global geopolitical scheme of things, Strauss felt that von Neumann's argument about the limits to science being determined by the limits to one's ability to carry out computation had deep national security implications. So despite having only the dimmest awareness of what these implications might actually be, Strauss wanted to ensure that whatever they were, the power of the computer stayed firmly in hands that he could monitor and control. That meant they should stay in von Neumann's hands at the IAS.

So as soon as the floor was open for discussion, Strauss jumped in to add,

"At our last meeting, we all heard Professor von Neumann tell us some of the reasons he feels so strongly about the computer project. I can tell you that privately he has told me even more than he said then. And what he said convinces me that this project is not just important for the advancement of science, but vitally important to the security of this country."

"What do you mean by that?" enquired one of the lawyers, a droopy-eyed Southerner who generally half dozed through these trustee meetings. "How can a machine that simply adds and subtracts numbers—albeit very quickly—have national security implications?"

"Let me give you an example," said Strauss, thinking that this lawyer was certainly not one of the sharpest pins in the cushion if, in light of the effect the atomic bomb had on America's position in the world just a couple of years earlier, he needed an explanation of how scientific advancements can determine the course of a country's fortunes. "Suppose you had a surefire method for predicting the weather. Do you think that would give you an advantage in military operations?" asked Strauss, staring at this small-town, country lawyer.

"Guess it probably would," drawled the lawyer in agreement.

"But predicting the weather faster than it unfolds is a mathematical problem involving *lots* of calculations, just as Johnny explained at our last meeting. And if you have the computing power you can do these calculations; otherwise, you can't. Now suppose, just suppose, you could use this information to modify or actually *control* the weather. If that's not something vital to the security of a country, I don't know what is. There may be some in this room who wouldn't worry a bit about giving the Russians the ability to drop a hurricane on Miami or a drought in Kansas. But I'm not one of them.

If anyone is going to have this kind of capability, I want it to be America."

Strauss made this rather gratuitous remark looking straight at Oppenheimer, whose pale-blue eyes returned the look with a glare chilling enough to reduce the room temperature to polar levels. But Oppie was not to be baited by the admiral into a public confrontation over their radically different positions on the Russians, national security, or the role of science in public affairs. In an attempt to use Strauss's argument to create a rapprochement between the supporters of the computer project and those who leaned against it, he said, "I believe Admiral Strauss has made a telling point in support of the IAS being the home of Johnny's project. This Institute is about cutting-edge intellectual endeavors, not simply polishing an existing apple to a brighter shine. No one on our faculty exemplifies this spirit more than Johnny. As the Director I believe we have a duty to support these goals of the Institute as laid down by its founders. I, therefore, stand fully behind what has just been said in support of having the computer project housed here at the IAS."

At this juncture Oppenheimer received a strong vote of support from an unexpected source. Frank Aydelotte, a mild-mannered Quaker who had been trained in English literature at Oxford and later became President of Swarthmore College, sat on the IAS board as a representative of the American academic establishment—but from the humanistic, not the scientific, side. So when he spoke up in support of von Neumann's avowedly scientific adventure, Oppenheimer took it as a sign from the cosmos to press forward to get the trustees behind the project while the momentum was still moving in his direction.

"Dr. Aydelotte speaks for all of us, I believe, when he says that this project is important not just for science, but for the Institute as well. If there are no objections, I suggest we take a vote on the project now and move this matter off our agenda. Do I hear a second?"

Immediately, from the murmur of voices around the table, someone seconded the motion. Oppenheimer began to hand out paper for the trustees to mark their votes. But as he was doing so, Strauss said loudly, "I don't think we need to have these ballots, Dr. Oppenheimer. My sense is that we can settle this with a simple show of hands. Does anyone object to that?"

In a roomful of tweedy academics, investment bankers, and sleepy lawyers, it was difficult for anyone to stand up to Strauss when he had his mind set on something. So it was hardly a surprise when nary a peep was heard against his suggestion. Shrugging his shoulders, Oppenheimer sat back resignedly and called for a show of hands.

"How many favor von Neumann's project being carried on here at the IAS?"

Several hands shot up immediately, including, of course, those of Strauss and Aydelotte. Seeing the way the wind was blowing, the remaining trustees—some grudgingly—slowly raised their hands; a majority was achieved, and the matter was settled.

"Fine," said Oppenheimer. "I will inform Johnny of the decision."

Just as the last word was out of Oppie's mouth, Aydelotte raised his hand with a question: "What about the financing of this project? We spoke only briefly about this at our last meeting. I'm sure it will involve hiring several engineers and technicians, not to mention requiring modification of physical space and acquisition of very specialized materials. Does von Neumann expect the Institute to pay for the people and equipment that will be required?"

Strauss fielded that enquiry without even blinking: "There are already commitments of funds and material, as well as expertise, from the military—the Navy, in particular.

And the Radio Corporation of America down the road has promised to supply much of the specialized hardware needed for the machine. So it should not be necessary for the Institute to dip into its own funds for this project; it will be financed one hundred percent from the outside."

Aydelotte nodded contentedly, but then added another surprise in response to Strauss's rosy picture. "That may be. Yet it is my experience that there's never enough money and things always cost double what you think they will. So I would like to formally propose that the IAS allocate $100,000 from its own resources for von Neumann to draw upon as a kind of emergency fund if and when he needs it."

"Seconded," someone immediately boomed from the back of the room.

"In favor?" asked Oppenheimer quickly while the mood seemed to be strongly in von Neumann's favor. Following a chorus of 'Ayes' from around the table, Oppie declared: "The matter is settled. The IAS will support the establishment of a computer project to be directed by Professor von Neumann. Moreover, the Institute will place $100,000 of its own funds at von Neumann's disposal to facilitate the project. Are we all agreed on that?"

Silence gives consent, thought Oppie, as he looked at the faces around the table. I'm eager to tell Johnny the good news, he thought. This project has been in limbo long enough, and I'm relieved that the IAS will not lose Johnny to another institution over an intellectual tempest in a teapot like this.

Turning his attention away from the board, Oppenheimer glanced down at his notes and declared, "Time is fleeting and we still have much to do today. I suggest we move on to our next agenda item."

EPILOGUE

J ohn von Neumann did finally get his computer. After the
Institute's Board of Trustees approved the project, work
began in early 1947 to construct a separate building on
the grounds behind the main Institute buildings to house the
effort. By spring of 1951 the machine was ready for use, even
though the formal dedication of the machine did not take
place until June 10, 1952. The first truly large-scale problem,
requiring several hundred hours of computing, was run to calculate some fluid-flow problem for the Los Alamos Laboratories, in the summer of 1951. The computer project was finally
closed down in 1958, and today the building that housed the
project is little more than a storage shed in the backyard of the
IAS.

As a strange footnote to the episode, after the computer

project ended, the IAS faculty passed a resolution stating that never again would there be an applied project at the Institute, a resolution that stands to this day. Readers can find an excellent account of the IAS computer project in the volume, *John von Neumann and the Origins of Modern Computing* by William Aspray (MIT Press, Cambridge, MA, 1990). Von Neumann died in 1957 of bone cancer, most likely caused by an overdose of radiation received while observing American atomic tests on Bikini Atoll in the early 1950s.

Kurt Gödel was finally promoted to Professor in the School of Mathematics in 1953 and spent the last 25 years of his life in this exalted status. By all accounts he was a conscientious and diligent faculty member who performed the administrative tasks of a Professor promptly and efficiently. Unfortunately, the later years of his life were marred by increasing paranoia, which eventually led to his refusal to eat for fear his food was poisoned. He died in 1978, having essentially starved himself to death. A short account of Gödel's life and work is given in the volume *Gödel: A Life of Logic* by John Casti and Werner DePauli (Perseus Books, Cambridge, MA, 2000). A somewhat more complete biography is the volume *Logical Dilemmas* by John Dawson (A.K. Peters, Wellesley, MA, 1997).

J. Robert Oppenheimer served as Director of the IAS from 1947 until his retirement in 1966. In 1953 he faced a major personal crisis when the federal government, at the instigation of President Eisenhower himself, withdrew Oppenheimer's security clearance on the grounds that "More probably than not, J. Robert Oppenheimer is an agent of the Soviet Union." The basis for this amazing claim was Oppenheimer's early communist associations. His brother Frank was an avowed communist. So was Frank's wife. And Oppenheimer's own wife, Kitty, had been a communist sympathizer in her youth. The government hearings on the withdrawal of Oppenheimer's security clearance split the scientific community of the day into those who were "with" Oppie and those who were "against." Many accounts of this brouhaha have been given, one of the most readable being the volume *Lawrence and Oppenheimer* by Nuel Pharr Davis (Simon and Schuster, New York, 1968).

Albert Einstein died in 1955, isolated from the very quantum revolution in physics that he created with his pathbreaking work on the photoelectric effect, in the early part of the twentieth century. The classical physicist's physicist, he never reconciled himself to the quantum credo that "A phenomenon is not a phenomenon until it is an observed phenomenon." With the sole exception of his 1935 paper with Podolsky and Rosen posing the quantum measurement paradox discussed in the text, it seems his life as a working physicist was over by the time he came to Princeton. So many accounts of every aspect of Einstein's life have been written that it would be pointless to list even one of them here. It would be hard to believe that any reader of this book has not encountered one or more of them.

The central philosophical issue of this story, the limits to scientific knowledge, remains as murky and unsettled as ever. Perhaps the difficulty lies in the very vagueness of the question. As soon as we try to define what is meant by "limits," "scientific," or "knowledge," everyday language fails us and we are immediately caught up in a plethora of semantic confusions. In contrast to the situation in mathematics, in which there is a well-defined notion of what it means to "decide" a question, in science there is no clear-cut concept of an *answer*.

Nevertheless, work continues on sharpening the issue, if not resolving it. A good account of the current state of affairs is the volume *Boundaries and Barriers,* edited by John Casti and Anders Karlqvist (Addison-Wesley, Reading, MA, 1996).